Napoleon Bona

The siege of Toulon

Charles James Fox

Alpha Editions

This edition published in 2019

ISBN : 9789353703363

Design and Setting By
Alpha Editions
email - alphaedis@gmail.com

NAPOLEON BONAPARTE

AND

THE SIEGE OF TOULON

INAUGURAL-DISSERTATION

ZUR

ERLANGUNG DER DOKTORWÜRDE

DER

HOHEN PHILOSOPHISCHEN FAKULTÄT

DER

RUPRECHT=KARLS=UNIVERSITÄT ZU HEIDELBERG

VORGELEGT VON

CHARLES JAMES FOX

AUS

BOSTON, MASS., U. S. A.

WASHINGTON, D. C.
LAW REPORTER COMPANY, PRINTERS.
1902.

CONTEMPORARY ACCOUNTS AND BIBLIOGRAPHY.

A. CONTEMPORARY ACCOUNTS.

Reports in:[1] Archives de la Guerre à Paris; Archives Nationales à Paris: Manuscript Department, British Museum: Public Record Office London.

Periodicals: Moniteur; The London Gazette; Gazeta de Madrid.

B. BIBLIOGRAPHY.

The Naval Chronicle, July to Dec. 1793. London, 1799.

Speeches of the Hon. W. Pitt 4 vols. London, 1806.

Speeches of the Hon. C. J. Fox 6 vols. London, 1815.

Précis historique sur les événements de Toulon, d'Imbert, Paris, 1814.

Notes et pièces officielles relatives aux événements de Marseilles et de Toulon, Abeille, Paris, 1815.

Revolution royaliste de Toulon, de Brecy, Paris, 1816.

Parliamentary History of England Vol 30. London, 1817.

Memoires pour servir à l'histoire de France sous Napoléon écrits à St. Hélène par Montholon 5 vols; par Gourgard 2 vols. Paris, 1823.

Memoires politiques et militaires du General Doppet 1 vol. Paris, 1824.

Memoires de Fréron Paris, 1824.

Memoires pour servir à l'histoire de la ville de Toulon en 1793, Pons, Paris, 1825.

Historie de la Revolution française Tome sixième Thiers, Paris, 1834.

Memoires du Prince de la Paix Don Manuel Godoy 4 vols. Paris, 1836.

Biographie de Napoléon Bonaparte, Coston, Paris, 1840.

---

[1] Many of the reports, especially in the Archives de la Guerre, are full of orthographical errors. I have copied them exactly as I found them.

Extraits de Memoires inédites du duc de Bellune, Paris, 1846.

Memoires de Claude Victor Perrin duc de Bellune Paris, 1847.

Life and correspondence of Admiral Sir W. Sidney Smith, Barrow 2 vols. London, 1848.

Memorials and correspondence of C. J. Fox, Russell London, 1853.

Correspondance de Napoléon Vol. 1. Paris, 1853.

Journal and correspondence of William Lord Auckland 4 vols. London, 1862.

Oestreich und Preussen gegenüber der Franzoesischen Revolution bis zum Abschluss des Friedens von Campio Formio, H. Hueffer, Bonn, 1868.

Memoires sur la guerre des Alpes tirés des papiers du Comte Ignas Thaon de Revel, Turin, Rom, Florence 1871.

Vertrauliche Briefe des Freiherren von Thugut, von Vivenot, Band I Vienna, 1872.

Life and Letters of Sir Gilbert Elliot first Earl of Minto, 1751 to 1806 3 vols. London, 1874.

Life of Thomas Graham Lord Lynedoch A. M. Delavoye London, 1880.

Bonaparte et son temps, 1769–99. 3 vols. Jung Paris, 1880–81.

Campaignes dans les Alpes pendant la Revolution 1792–93 Krebs et Morris, Paris, 1891.

Recueil des actes du Comité de Salut Public avec la correspondance officielle des representants en mission. F. A. Aulard Paris, 1894.

Memoires de Barras 4 vols. Duruy Paris, 1895–6.

The manuscripts of J. B. Fortesque Esq. Vol. 2 London, 1894.

Napoléon Bonaparte et les Généraux Du Teil, Baron Joseph du Teil, Paris, 1897.

Toulon et les Anglais en 1793. Paul Cottin Paris, 1898.

La Jeunesse de Napoléon, Chuquet Paris, 1899.

PREFACE.

The siege of Toulon in 1793 is interesting and important, as a military event in the War of the First Coalition; as a political combination of the European Powers during the early part of the same war; and as a personal incident in the life of Napoleon Bonaparte. The following pages are the result of a study of the siege in which I have tried to give special attention to the second and third phases of the question. I have come to the conclusion that the political importance of the siege was considerable and that the English entered Toulon unexpectedly and intended to hold it simply as a pledge of indemnification; and secondly that the role of Bonaparte was very important and that he by directing the course of this siege, had here for the first time an influence upon the events of his time and consequently enters history. As the last point has been much disputed and as the others have not yet been brought out, I have in attempting to demonstrate each, given as much as possible of the material used, together with frequent references, allowing him whom the subject may interest to draw his own conclusions, hoping however that they will coincide with those which in my opinion are the logical and just ones.

The first accounts of Napoleon's actions were written during, and under the influence of, the grandeur of the Consulate and First Empire. The part he played at Toulon was generally considered great and brilliant; but this prevalent opinion was based principally upon more or less inexact reminiscences of those who took part in the siege with him. Everybody accepted without going into particulars that the First Consul, or Emperor, began his career at Toulon, where his genius first attracted attention. At the Restauration royalists who had served at Toulon published accounts of the siege, which with regard to the role of Bonaparte, had rather the opposite tendency. But as their principal aim was to

bring forward their own actions and thereby win the favor
of Louis XVIII, and as anti-Bonapartist statements needed
then no foundation on fact, these writings are of no ob-
jective value. They reflect but the anti-Bonapartist and
pro-English sentiment of the Court at this time. Thiers
throws some light on Bonaparte's role at Toulon, attributing
principally to him the fall of the city; but Thiers' Work was
to vast to permit him to make any special study of the affair of Toulon. His account of it is filled with errors. The
Memoirs of Barras (not published until 1895) furnish ample
but quite untrustworthy material to those who wish to les-
sen the role of Bonaparte at this siege. This same spirit of
hostility to Napoleon prevails in Jung's "Bonaparte et son
temps" He too denies the importance of the role of Bonaparte at Toulon but he does not go much into particulars,
nor did he study the question without prejudice. The eager-
ness with which he seeks an opportunity of defaming the
name of Bonaparte is shown where he himself speaks of
Napoleon (page 372 vol. I) as an officer of 25 years when he
wrote the "Souper de Beaucaire", and then again deliber-
ately accuses him (page 396) of giving a false age in stating
that he was 25 after the siege of Toulon. Krebs and Morris
in their work on Campagnes in the Alpes give a good general account of the siege, but the role of Bonaparte is passed
by with the mere assertion that in the official records nothing is found to prove its importance. It is true that in the
documents of the Archives de la Guerre at Paris, no direct
statement can be found that Napoleon Bonaparte took a
very important part in the entire affair; but indirect proofs
are by no means wanting, either here or in the English official reports. The two latest works on Toulon are those of
Cottin and Chuquet. Cottin leaves the role of Bonaparte
rather aside and using the English sources, writes on their
action at Toulon. His work has the value of publishing important documents hitherto inaccessible in printed form;
but with the same he has combined much doubtful detail

derived from rather untrustworthy and contradictory
sources. His book has an anti-English tendency and fails to
bring out the political importance of the affair of Toulon.
Chuquet's work, an enlargement of two articles published in
Cosmopolis, is of rather a popular character but it publishes
for the first time some letters of Bonaparte and other important pieces. He goes into detail which is very difficult to
control and the sources of which he has not always carefully considered. The role of Bonaparte is emphasized, but
not in a manner convincing enough for a question so much
in dispute.

In publishing this small volume I wish to take advantage of the opportunity to express my sincere gratitude to
all my Professors at Heidelberg, and to mention my appre-
ciation of the kindness of the late Professor Erdmannsdörf-
fer and Professor Schäfer, whose generous aid and hospitality
to foreigners I shall always try to emulate.

PART I.

CONDITIONS UNDER WHICH TOULON SUR-
RENDERED TO THE ENGLISH AND
SIEGE OF TOULON.

CHAPTER I.

FRANCE IN 1793—TOPOGRAPHICAL DESCRIPTION OF TOU-
LON—NEGOTIATIONS PRECEEDING SURRENDER—PROC-
LAMATION OF HOOD—HOOD'S ENTRANCE—ARRIVAL OF
NEWS IN LONDON—POLITICAL SITUATION OF ALLIES AT
TIME OF SIEGE—OPINIONS ON HOOD'S DECLARATION—
ENGLISH IDEA AS TO RETENTION OF TOULON.

In 1793 the French Revolution had advanced far in its
impetuous course. In its commencement ill defined, its
course hard to foresee, and uncertain, it had at its culmina-
tion formed itself into a definite, cruel and reckless system,
the Terror. Power had passed from the right to the extreme
left of the National Assembly, and there into hands which
were capable of holding and using it. The execution of
Louis XVI, the crowning act of the Revolution took place
at the beginning of this year; shortly after followed the re-
volt in the Vendée: the first attempt at military rule was de-
feated as Dumouriez went over to the Austrians: the Giron-
dists were overthrown by their more reckless and energetic
rivals: then followed the uprising of two-thirds of the de-
partments and of many large cities, Lyons, Marseilles, Toulon and Bordeaux. The situation in the interior of France
was very uncertain, and the dangers from without were
great. After Neerwinden Belgium was lost and the Austrians
advanced victoriously into Northern France. The Prussians
retook Mayence and put an end to its revolutionary exces-
ses. The Piedmontese forced their way over the Alps, the
Spaniards came over the Pyrenees. The English were everywhere on the seas. It was under these conditions that France,
or more strictly Revolutionary France, stood alone against
the nations of Europe united in the pursuit of their different political ambitions, and in the hope of future advantages. For whatever may have been the origin of the Revo-

2192—1

lutionary Wars, the European nations, once united against France, were striving after their own interests, and these at the expense of France, who at this time seemed inevitably lost. This however was not the case. Everyone knows the Peace of Campio Formio which followed that of Basel and others, yet it is by no means easy to explain clearly how the Republicans performed the seemingly impossible and forced upon the entire Continent such advantageous terms. The history of the Siege of Toulon gives an insight into these conditions, for one might almost say that here the War of the First Coalition took place on a smaller scale. The same forces stood opposing each other. On the one side, the European powers, England, Spain, Sardinia, Naples even Austria, as well as the French Royalists and Emigres; on the other the enthusiastic, almost fanatical, self-sacrificing, but uncertain Republican army, directed by a few ingenious leaders, among them Bonaparte and Victor, and supported at home by an active energetic government under the organizing genius of Carnot. Everything was sacrificed to the object of the war. On the one side was discord, distrust, jealousy, and ill-directed egotism. The best energy of the European nations exhausted itself over the division of spoils which were still to be won. On the other side was geographic and political unity, together with a fanatical devotion to the one object. All passions, the ambition of the demagogue and of the soldier, even the fear of the Republicans, lead to the same end; namely, the liberating of France from the foreign invader. On the one hand it was a question of obtaining certain advantages, in the distribution of which lay the cause of future disagreement; on the other, it was a question of life and death; and this struggle for existence was carried on by energetic reckless men who had risen by their own force and ability, and who in the choice of thier means were unhampered by any traditional, religious or even human considerations.

To understand a siege it is necessary, first to have an idea

of the topographical and other military conditions of the
place in which it is carried on. In the year 1793 Toulon,
a city of some 28,000 inhabitants, was enclosed by a circle
of fortifications which dated from the time of Vauban, but
which had been continually improved and were now in
fairly good condition. It was reputed one of the strongest
fortifications in Europe. On the land side Toulon is surrounded by high mountains especially the massive ridge of
Mount Faron on the north. From the city one road leads to
Marseilles and another eastward toward Italy. The Rivière
Neuve flows from the north past the western side of the
city, into the inner of the two harbors, which are called the
Grande and Petite Rade. This river is dry in the summer.
The fortifications on the north-west were Fort Pomets and
the Redoute St. Andre (completed but not armed); on the
north-east, Fort Rouge, Fort Blanc, and the intrenched
camp, Ste. Anne. Mont Faron also protected the city on the
north. On the east, to defend the road to Italy was Fort La
Malgue. According to Napoleon, this fort was very carefully
built. It protected also the Grande Rade. Fort Ste. Catherine
and Fort L'Artigues, likewise on the east, were supported
by Mont Faron. On the west was Fort Malbousquet. It
was merely a temporary fortification, but important through
its position. Fort Missiessy was also on the west, on the
north shore of the Petite Rade. The entrance to the Grande
Rade was covered by Fort La Malgue, that of the Petite
Rade by Fort Grosse Tour, on the eastern side, and by the
coast batteries, Balaguier and Eguillette, on the western
side. In general, more importance had been placed on the
fortifications on the east of the city than on those on the
west. It was supposed that all attacks were to come from
the Italian side.

In Toulon, as in most of the cities and many of the De-
partments, there was a revolutionary and a Royalist party,
each striving to obtain power. In Toulon the Republicans
found support in the Republican army under Carteaux.

The Royalists, in accordance with their policy at that time, sought help from outside. [1] The English squadron had been seen for weeks before Toulon, where her Admiral, Lord Hood, stood watching the large French fleet in the harbor. To destroy this formed part of his plan; which was to win and hold for England the supremacy of the Mediterranean. The Royalists of Marseilles and Toulon were in constant communication, and were secretly forming plans. A certain undecided portion of the population was to be won over to their side. For some time they cherished the plan of inviting the English to enter. In some manner the English representative in Turin, John Trevor, who was well informed on the affairs of Italy and the Mediterranean, got news of this intention and wrote as early as July 21 to Hood, informing him of the possibility of an appeal for help from the people of Toulon. Hood seemed, however, to have given the matter but little attention. His object was still the French fleet. A few days before, on July 19, he had sent a Lieutenant Cook into Toulon to negotiate an exchange of prisoners; permitting him to wait twenty-four hours for a reply.

Cook returned bringing with him a list of the French ships in Toulon, and other useful information. It is possible, although all evidence is wanting, that Cook, who was Hood's nephew, entered even at this time, into communication with the Royalists. The Royalists resorted to a trick to win over the still undecided portion of the inhabitants. The fear of a bread famine was held out before the people; although there were provisions for three months at hand. Thaon de Revel, the commander of the Piedmontese troops wrote: "L'appréhension de la famine fut la consideration qui décida les habitans. Les chefs avaient persuadé à la multitude que bientôt elle manquerait de pain si l' on ne

---

[1] de Brécy. "Un sentiment presque unanime inspira le projet d'envoyer un parlementaire au commandant anglais pour lui demander son concours et son assistance."

traitait avec les Anglais; quoique dans le fait il y eut du grain pour plus de trois mois." [1] Nelson, who at the time of the siege, was sailing in and out of the harbor of Toulon, wrote " Famine had done what force could not have done." [2] In this manner the people were deceived and won over. Negotiations with Hood commenced first from Marseille, then from Toulon, the latter being of much more interest to the English. At first one spoke of an importation of grain into Marseille, finally of the conditional surrender of Toulon to the English.

After holding a Council of War Hood gave out, on August 23, a preliminary declaration, which was soon followed by a proclamation. Both were sent to Marseille and Toulon. The declaration said : That if the people of Toulon and Marseille declare openly for monarchy; if the vessels are disarmed and the harbor and forts put provisionally in Hood's charge, the people of Provence may count upon the assistance of the British fleet: the rights of property and of the individual shall be protected : further, that Hood's only object is the restoration of peace and that then all will be returned " conformément à l'inventaire qui en sera fait ". In the Proclamation Hood gives a " tableau fièdle " of the " malheureuse condition " of the French nation during the last four years, and declares that the European nations see no remedy to such evils other than reestablishment of monarchy in France. He offers his protection and aid to establish " un gouvernment regulier et de maintainir la paix et la tranquillité dans l'Europe." Hood's proclamation arrived too late in Marseilles; the approaching Republican army made it impossible to continue the negociations. In Toulon the most stormy debates took place in the Sections when Lieutenant Cook announced Hood's offer. The Royalists carried off the victory, in spite of all opposition of the other party, and of the hostile attitude of the French ships in

[1] Memoirs.
[2] Letters Sept. 14th. Nelson dispatches.

the harbor. The Sections decided for the entrance of the English, but under several conditions. Among others; the present constitution was to be replaced by the monarchical government, under the Constitution of 1791;[1] civil and military officers were to retain their places. The provisioning of the city was to be assured; an inventory was to be made of the vessels and of all material in the port. These conditions were carried back by Cook to Hood, who accepted them. His present fleet was however not strong enough to risk entering alone. He therefore asked assistance from the Spanish Admiral Langara who at first refused, but consented on a second invitation from Hood, who accompanied this invitation with a copy of his intended proclamation. In the meantime Hood published his second proclamation to the inhabitants of Toulon. It was dated August 28th and declared: 'as the Sections of Toulon have declared Louis XVII as their legitimate sovereign and for monarchy according to the constitution of 1791, he takes possession of Toulon and will guard it "en dépôt pour Louis XVII jusqu' au rétablissement de la paix en France".

The next day as the Spanish fleet appeared in sight Hood sailed into the harbor, the Spanish following.[2] The seamen of the French fleet were divided into two parties, the Jacobins and the Royalists. The first showed in the beginning a determination to oppose the landing of the English, but were held in check by the Royalists and the land batteries. Finally, threatened by the English and Spanish, they found it better to take advantage of a chance to escape, than to offer resistance. The crew of seven ships succeeded in getting away. Hood and Langara received a most enthusiastic reception from the inhabitants and officials of Toulon. An excellent understanding existed between the two ad-

---

[1] This constitution was always referred to, and is spoken of in the following pages, as the constitution of 1789.

[2] Journal of Samuel Lord Hood. Admiralty Records. Public Record Office.

mirals. A thousand marines and about 300 sailors from each fleet were landed immediately at Fort LaMalgue.[1]

On September 12th the news of the fall of Toulon reached London by way of Turin. It caused in government circles quite as much surprise as satisfaction. It was decided to collect troops and send them to Hood without deranging the plans of campaign in general. The first intention was to send 5000 British troops, raised in Ireland, and 5000 Hessians.[2] As early as September 14th, and at Pitt's suggestion,[3] instructions were sent to Sir Morton Eden, the English ambassador at Vienna to ask for Austrian troops. These were promised, but never arrived. More about the negociations concerning the will be given later.

Here it might be well to insert an account of the political situation of Europe at this time. Three important questions preoccupied more or less, the different cabinets. The war against the Republic, affairs in Poland and Austria's resumed plan of exchanging the Netherlands for Bavaria. Nearly all the nations were joined in the struggle with France but the attention of several of them Austria, Prussia, Russia, an others was much diverted by the other two questions. The news of the second division of Poland brought Thugut, whose anti-Prussian policy was well known, into power in Vienna. An understanding between Austria and England was the result. This power, (England) as well as the other European nations, now taking for granted, (and under existing conditions it was almost pardonable) that France would fall, directed its best thoughts and energy to her future dismemberment, and to its share of the "Indemnification." The plans of the English government, having taken rather a definite form, full instructions were sent to

[1] Letter from Graham to Sir William Hamilton. Correspondence. British Museum. Manuscript Department. Egerton 2638.

[2] Letter Dundas to Sir James Murray. Sept. 14. War Office. British Army on Continent. 1793. Record Office.

[3] Letter Pitt to Grenville. Sept 7. Manuscripts of J. B. Fortescue.

Eden in Vienna. They were dated Whitehall. Sept. 7.[1] and contained, first, an account of Austria's plans, as they have been stated in England, namely "the making permanent acquisitions, to as large an extent as they are practicable, in the Low Countries, in Alsace and Loraine, and in the intermediate parts of the frontier of France. No similar communication has as yet been made on the part of His Majesty, but the circumstances and situation of affairs have made it sufficiently evident that whatever indemnification is to be acquired by this country must be looked for in the foreign settlements and colonies of France. In these objects the interest of the two Courts are so far from clashing that His Majesty has an interest in seeing the House of Austria strengthen itself by acquisition on the French frontier, and the very circumstance of that interest should make the Emperor see with pleasure the relative increase of the naval and commercial resources of this country beyond those of France. . . . . As to the Powers who are already engaged in the war it does not appear that much can be done by Austria, at least in the present moment towards securing the co-operation of Spain. But no endeavours will be omitted by His Majesty for that purpose ". . . . In speaking of the coolness between Austria and Sardinia, "the idea once entertained by the Court of Vienna of extending the frontier of the Milanese at the expense of the King of Sardinia is, I trust, abandoned, but if brought forward again, must be strongly discouraged by you " . . . . As regards Prussia, "it is obvious that the interest of the Emperor is as much concerned as that of His Majesty in securing even at the expense of some sacrifice the co-operation and assistance of the King of Prussia. If no step is taken to remove the increasing jealousy between those two courts the worst consequences may be expected from them " . . . . Then follows advice to Austria to renounce her

---

[1] Foreign Office. Austria. Sir Morton Eden. Aug. to Oct. 93. Public Record Office.

claim on Bavaria in order to avoid Prussia's jealousy. The Elector might then take an active part in the war, might send troops to His Majesty "who would not be unwilling to incur a considerable expense for an object of so much importance to the common cause." . . . . As to Russia, "His Majesty's endeavours to obtain the active co-operation of that power have proved ineffective. The assistance of a body of troops having ultimately been refused to His Majesty except on terms which, independant of other objections, would have committed this country with respect to the interior of France beyond what His Majesty judged to be advisable or prudent." . . . . "In the Mediterranean the interests of this country are, that our naval superiority over France should be maintained and there is no reason to doubt of this point being sufficiently secured" . . . . Here Grenville mentions the necessity of the assistance of 12 or 15,000 Austrian troops for affairs in the Mediterranean. . . . "I have mentioned to you His Majesty's disposition to connect himself by a defensive alliance with the Emperor, and I have stated that you are at liberty to give the strongest assurances on this head. The basis of such an alliance would naturally be, as I have explained to Count Starhenberg the same with of the ancient system by which the two countries were formally united: the securing a barrier against France, the retaining the Netherlands under the lawful sovereignty of Austria, the securing and augmentation of the commerce of the Maritime Powers, and the Mutual guaranty of all possessions antecedent to the war."

The foregoing instructions give an insight into political relations at this moment. The following extract from a letter to Grenville, from Lord St. Helens, the English Ambassador at Madrid, completes it to some extent. [1] It was dated Madrid, August 28. "I understand that the Duke of Alcudia

---

[1] Foreign Office. Spain. Lord St. Helens and Consuls' dispatches Aug. to Dec. 1793. Public Record Office.

·has testified a great deal of Pique and Dissatisfaction to the Prussian and Austrian Ministers on account of the late capitulations of Mentz and Valanciennes concerning that from the vague and indefinite terms they were drawn the French government will consider themselves as at liberty to employ these garrisons in their armies on this Frontier. There appears great reason to hope that these alarms may prove groundless. However this seeming want of attention to the interests of this crown on the part of the Emperor and the King of Prussia has increased the sentiments of jealousy against those sovereigns, which have been so long entertained here, and which I observe to be studiously kept up and inflamed by the agents of the French Princes. With regard to England, the Spanish Minister's language is still friendly and cordial, however, I am told that some ill-intentioned Persons have been endeavouring to persuade him that we have acted un-candidly by this Court in concluding a Treaty with Naples without their knowledge, and I therefore take the liberty of submitting to your Lordship whether if that Treaty contained nothing of a secret nature it might not be advisable to communicate it here without loss of time " . . . .

Here is the political situation in a few words. England looked for indemnification outside of Europe; an increase of her commerce and supremacy over France in the Mediterranean. Her object was to bring the war to a fortunate termination and for that reason to hold the European nations together. She was willing to make financial sacrifices for the common cause. She would not commit herself as to the future government in France. Austria wished to increase her possessions in the Netherlands and in Alsace; she was jealous of Prussia. She hoped also to extend her Milanese territory, and there was jealousy between her and Sardinia. She was not quite so decided about continuing her plan of obtaining Bavaria. Spain had cause of ill-will against Austria and Prussia. Russia continued her policy of refraining from any active part in the war against France. England had signed treaties with Sardinia, [1] Naples, Hesse and Baden, by which they agreed to furnish her troops. Prussia's attention was turned toward Poland and she was already wavering in her policy of war against the Republic.

The English government was not quite satisfied with Lord Hood's declaration. Grenville wrote to Eden Sept. 14. [2] "Lord Hood has been induced by circumstances and by the great advantage which was in view, to go further with respect to the Interior state of France and to the Futur Government to be established there, than was in contemplation according to the ideas stated to you in my late dispatch. You will explain the circumstances to the Austrian Minister and you will add that on this account as well as from the Change which the event of Toulon produced in our situation it may perhaps be advisable that some public measure should be taken on this subject by this court, and that of Vienna jointly. The ideas on this subject which are entertained by His Majesty's Ministers will be transmitted to you with as little delay as possible." In Spain the news of Toulon's surrender was well received. St. Helens wrote to Grenville, Sep 6. [3] "I need not say that this court are highly satisfied with these advices, and above all with Lord Hood's invitation tŏ Admiral Langara to partake in his success, and that they profess the utmost readiness to co-operate with us cordially in every step of the business." The news of Hood's entrance was also welcomed by the Royalists and Emigrants, and for a time it was supposed that other cities would follow the example of Toulon. In the information sent to the For-

---

[1] Letter Dundas to O'Hara. 18th Dec. Letters from Secry. Dundas to Lieut. Gen. Dundas. 1793–94. British Museum. Mss. Dept. Additional 27,594.

"By treaty 26. April. Sardinian Majesty in consequence of payment of subsidy has bound himself to furnish his majesty 20,000 troops free of any further expense."

[2] Public Record Office.

[3] St. Helens. Public Record Office.

eign Office; dated Sept 20. [1] one reads "On croit que les Royalistes à Brest dont il y a grand nombre feront en sorte que la flotte renterra sous peu de jours et qu'on y proclamera comme à Toulon Louis 17 " . . . . De Saint Croix, one of the Emigrants in London, wrote to Grenville, dated London, Sept. 15. [1] " Lorsque j'eus avant hier l'honneur d'écrire à Votre Excellence je ne connaissais point les deux proclamations de M. L'Amiral Hood. Permettez-moi mi-lord de vous en exprimer et comme français et comme individu toute ma reconnaissance. Puissent tous les cabinets adopter ce language: il y a plus de gloire à parler ainsi qu'à vaincre. . . . Vous nous rendez Mylord quelque confience et quelque sécurité: vous commandez l'estime de l'Europe et vous lui donnez un grand exemple."

The opinion in England was somewhat divided as to the advisability of retaining Toulon, even temporarily, but all were united in rejoicing that the French fleet was in English hands. It was even suggested that upon a good opportunity it might be burned and the town given up. As the seige went on it was not hard to see that the question of what was to be done with the French fleet became a most delicate one. It was partly upon this point that the difference arose between the English and Spanish Admirals, and later their respective Governments. Lord Sheffield wrote September 15th to Auckland [2] "I see no use of encumbering ourselves with Toulon unless we carry home the French fleet. I should certainly have taken advantage of the kind of resistance made by the French fleet, by hauling into the inner road and would have burnt them all to save further embarrassment." Pitt speaks of the taking of Toulon as a " most fortunate event." [3] The Marquis of Buckingham wrote to Grenville Sept 15. " We have only to pray that the

---

[1] Foreign Office. Domestic Papers. March to Dec. 1793. Public Record Office.

[2] Auckland Papers. British Museum. Mss. vol 12. Additional 34,452.

[3] Letter to Grenville. Sept 7. Manuscripts of Fortescue.

patriots may besiege Toulon and that the issue of the contest may be the conflagration of the docks and fleet."[1] And on Sept 29th. "You must be prepared to meet much opposition to the idea of indemnification which the emigrants now in London are loud in reprobating. At the same time the people of Brest and Toulon can not be very anxious for the slices which may be required from France on the side of the Pays Bas and of Lorain, or even of Piedmont; and whether they are or no it is good to habituate people early to the sound of such a proposition"[1] . . . . on Oct. 4th. "I conclude that our fleet winters at Toulon and refits with *French stores taken upon a valuation*; but at all events, I hope that you will retain the superiority in those seas even over the Spaniards, whose operations except those of Langara do not please me"[1] Nelson wrote Oct. 7th. "Whether we shall be able to maintain our most extraordinary acquisition time only can determine, however one hour will burn the French fleet"[2] . . . . The plan of D' Alcudia, the Spanish minister was [3] that the combined squadrons should seize the first opportunity of forcibly removing all the Toulon ships to some place of greater security, as Port Mahon or Carthagena.

When the Comité du Salut Public heard of the surrender of Toulon they sent off the following laconic note to the "Representants du Peuple" with the Republican army at Toulon. "Citoyens collègues . . Nous avons appris avec indignation la perfide trahison de Toulon dont vous nous informez par votre dépêche du 29 (sic) Août: du courage, de la fermeté de la constance: nous vaincrons les royalists, les despots et les traitres."[4]

---

[1] Letter to Grenville. Sept. 7. Manuscripts of Fortescue.
[2] Nelson Dispatches.
[3] St. Helens. to Grenville Oct. 2. Record Office.
[4] Reponse du Comité. Aug. 28. Re cueil Aulard.

CHAPTER II.

Carteaux, the Republican General, entered Marseilles on
August 25. [1] He did not march directly on Toulon as he
was waiting for reinforcements from the army of Italy, which
were approaching from the east, nor did he dare leave Marseilles unprotected. Toulon was threatened from the east and
west by two armies, just as the allies arrived. The English
especially were ill prepared in a military way, having no
soldier of a higher rank than captain. [2] It was impossible to
do much towards fortifying the town, which, especially on
the western side, where the French had never expected an
attack, was rather exposed. One feared somewhat a "coup
de main" by Carteaux, aided by the discontented in the
town, of which there were a large number. From the beginning the Republicans were not idle. "Nous avons donné
l'ordre de faire sonner le tocsin dans toutes les communes
du départment du Var et de faire marcher tous les citoyens
depuis l'âge de 16 ans jusqu'à 60". This shows a praise-
worthy activity, but to allow such crowds to be hurled by
incompetant generals against a fortified city was worse than
foolish.

---

[1] Lettre de Salicetti. Aug 25. R. A.

[2] Letter. T. Graham to Sir William Hamilton. British Museum. Mss.
Egerton. 2638. (14)

Carteaux's advance guard occupied the passes of Ollioules on the 29th of August. The English and Spanish hearing of it, promptly drove the Republicans back. This was the first action and there were but a few casualties. This position however, was important, as it commanded the road to Marseilles, and also the communications with La Seyne, a village on the south-west corner of the Petite Rade; but it was too far from Toulon for the Allies to hold it in their present condition. Carteaux who had just (Sept 4.) been appointed to the command of the beseiging army, [1] which was to be independant of the army of Italy, made preparations to retake it. On September 7. the attack took place and was successful. [2] The Allies retreated to the town with a small loss: the Republicans lost but one man, and Donmartin, who commanded the artillery was severely wounded. This slight success of the Republicans caused a somewhat bad impression in the town. The Republicans now closed in from the east and west. Carteaux, who commanded the western division in person, established his head-quarters at Ollioules and extended his position from Faubrégas to Baon-de-Quatres-Heures. Lopoype, who had come from the Italian Army, commanded on the east. His head-quarters were at Solliès-Farlède. Lapoype was an ex-marquis whose Jacobinisme was much less to questioned than his ability as a general. He was not much inferior to Carteaux however, especially in this kind of military work. His wife was a prisoner in Toulon and this fact hampered him in his movements.[3] The Republicans were very weak in artillery, and some of it had to be left in Marseille " pour foudroyer cette ville s'il s'y manifestait quelque mouvement." Now they were even deprived of their chief of artillery, Donmartin. With the material at hand however, Carteaux had erected a battery on the

---

[1] Armée du Siege de Toulon. Archives de la guerre.

[2] Lettre de Carteaux à Lapoype. Sept 8. Archives de la guerre. Lettre Capt. Cook to Gen. Ed. Smith. Sept 7. Barrow's life of Sidney Smith.

[3] Lapoype à Bouchotte. Sept 11. Archives de la Guerre.

west side, to burn the fleet: but its position, far out of range of either the fleet or town, was laughable.[1] Reinforcements continued to arrive on each side and both parties prepared themselves for the struggle. Spain was especially prompt in sending reinforcements.[2] By returns taken on Sep 12. [3] there were over 5000 troops and sailors on shore: of these 3400 were Spanish and about 1600 English. This force quite exceeded that of Carteaux in efficiency and probably in numbers. Hood wrote on Sept 14 the "Enemy not yet provided with artillery." The hopes of the Allies might well rise, for who could have suspected, unless it was the young Corsican himself, and at this very moment the besieging army had received a most formidable reinforcement?

On September 16 or 17 [4] the direction of the principal

---

[1] Carteaux a Lopoype. Sept 8.

[2] Letters from St. Helens. Sept 18. Record Office

[3] Letter from St. Helens Sept 25. R. O.
Graham to Hamilton. Sept 14.
Correspondence. British Museum. Mss.
Egerton. 2638.

[4] The exact date when Napoleon arrived in Toulon is difficult to place. He says in his Memoires the 12th. of Sept. Chuquet believes he has proved that he arrived on the 16th. of Sept. (Page 171—note) "On ignorait jusqu'ici le jour où Bonaparte arriva devant Toulon. Ses mémoires disent tantôt le 12 Sept. tantot douze à quinze jours après la prise d'Ollioules, du 19 au 22 Septembre. Mais il est sûrement le 15 à Marseille (cf. pièce LXIX ; a letter from Marseille, dated Sept 15) et, suivant une lettre de Salicetti, il fait le 17 à Ollioules les préparatifs d'une attaque ; il est donc arrivé le 16 au quartier général du Beausset. N' ecrit-il pas d'ailleurs pendant les siège " les batteries furent établies trois jours après son arrivée?" Or la batterie de la Montagne date du 19 Septembre." In the first place the contradiction in Napoleon's Memoirs can be explained. There are accounts of Toulon in two volumes written by different Generals. According to the First volume Napoleon arrived 12 or 15 days after the taking of Ollioules, which according to this volume took place on Sept 10 The arrival of Bonaparte would therefore have taken place between the 22nd and 25th of Sept, and not the 19th and 22nd as Chuquet puts it. This volume was corrected by Napoleon, but he probably gave no great attention to such details. The third volume was dictated by Napoleon and contains a twice as lengthy account of Toulon. Here he says expressly that he arrived on the 12th of Sept.

As to the date of the battery La Montagne, Chuquet gives it (page

arm of Carteaux's army was put under the control of Napoleon Bonaparte, then 24 years of age, and a captain of Artillery. A new period in Napoleon's life began here. In after
years when he was preoccupied about his own history, he
wished that it should begin with the siege of Toulon. This
is seen especially in his Memoirs from St. Helena. It is
usually said that in so doing his object was to pass over the
preceding period in Corsica, which would not tend to make
him popular in France. This may no doubt be partially
true, but it is none the less so that these three months, before the walls of Toulon, were three of the most important
in his life. Here his entire career was changed. Others besides himself were convinced of his ability, even of his genius.
He was thrown into close contact with the French people;
and became at last one of them. His ambition was freed
from the little island of Corsica, and bound itself to the des-
tinies of the French nation; soon afterwards to control them.

---

172) as Sept. 9., then (page 179) as Sept 12, and finally (page 206) Sep-
18. The evening of the 17th is the proper date, as on the morning of the
18th the battery fires on the ships. (Hood's Journal) On the 16th Dommartin was still, at least nominally, head of the artillery (Carteaux à
Lapoype, Archives de la Guerre) and on the 17th Napoleon directs it.
(Lettre Salicetti—Sept 26. R. A.) Salicetti writes "nous arrêtâmes le
citoyen Buonaparte et nous lue ordonnâmes de remplacer Dommartin".
It is quite possible that Napoleon was employed for a few days about
Toulon before he received Dommartin's position. He must have first
proved his ability to the Representants; or have influenced them in some
way (he knew Salicetti) before receiving the position which should otherwise have fallen to Lieut-colonel Sugney, who commanded the artillery
under Lapoype. It is a significant fact that on Sept 16, Carteaux writes
to Lapoype, "c'est l'artillerie qui fait toute la besogne", as if it were a
fact of which he has just become convinced: also in direct contradiction
to his previous ideas. Napoleon may have arrived on the 12th and yet
have returned to Marseilles on the 15th. If he did not arrive until the 16th
then his statement that he found almost no artillery, is incorrect, because just at this time some artillery at least begins to arrive. (Carteaux à
Lapoype, Sept 16. A. G.) Napoleon probably forwarded it himself from
Marseille where he was employed at the arsenal. By the September 19 Carteaux is aiding him as he writes to Bonaparte (Letter, A. G.) "Je viens
de recevoir votre lettre et je vais envoyer à la Municipalite pour vous
procurer tous les objets que vous me demandez".

2192—2

At the end of these three months he was no longer a ne-glected captain but a young general with a career behind him, as well as a far greater and more definite one before him. He had had an insight into the world of that day, and understood the political situation of his time. The means by which he was to satisfy his ambition were no longer vague dreams of the imagination but definite and deep-laid plans founded on an experience of men and a knowledge of conditions. His actions in Corsica must have now appeared to him as youthful. Feeling that he had matured in these three months it was no wonder that he should have believed that his career commenced at Toulon.

When Napoleon arrived he found the army in a most pitiable state; very little artillery [1] and what there was placed in a position harmless to the enemy;[2] the Generals without a plan, or rather with a new one each day, but most of them useless.[3] The staff did not even have a map of the town and surrounding country.[4] Napoleon saw what any other in-structed officer would have seen, that the first object was to attack the fleet in the harbor, and soon selected the best po-sition for doing so. He set to work immediately but before long he had a misunderstanding with Carteaux, who knew little about artillery. However, Bonaparte had very wisely as-sured himself of the all-powerful Representants du Peuple; with one of these, Salicetti, a Corsican, he had been in per-sonal connection before. In fact, in September Salicetti had caused Napoleon's brother Joseph to be appointed Commis-saire de Guerre with the rank of Lieutenant-Colonel.

These representants du peuple were characteristic of this period of the Revolution. Sent out to the armies and into

---

[1] Letter from Barras, 6 Sept. R. A.
    "   "   Lapoype to Carteaux Sept. 14, A. G.
[2] Letter from Albitte 9 Sept. R. A.
[3] Letter from Lapoype to Bouchotte, 11 Sept. A. G.
    "   "   Carteaux to Lapoype—14 Sept. A. G.
    "   "   "   to Mtre. de la Guerre—15 Sept. A. G.
[4] Carteaux au Ministere de la Guerre, Sept 12 and Sept 15. A. G.

the cities by the Central Government, their duty was to
watch the Generals, spur them on, and excite the patriotism
of the people; also to send frequent information to the Government in Paris. They were all powerful, and at the same
time quite independent. All mistakes were attributed to the
Generals, for whom the guillotine was not an unusual pen-
alty; the representants simply appointed new ones in their
places. They incorporated the idea of the absolute supremacy of the civil power over military and all other. No other
instances of a similar character are found in history. Salicetti, Barras, Gasparin, Albitte and others were at Toulon;
Salicetti during the entire siege. Little they suspected that
the young artillery officer, who courted their favor, flattered
their pride, and won their confidence, would in a few years
change the face of things, overturn the despotism of the
demagogue, and erect in its place a quite as despotic military power but less unjust, creative and lawgiving. The
beginning of this transition was seen in the Italian campaign of 1796–97, when General Clark sent out to watch
the young General Bonaparte, decided to cast in his lot with
Napoleon rather than with the Directory. Napoleon got
an excellent insight into the ways of these representatives
at Toulon, which no doubt aided him much in winning
over Clark.

On September 17 [1] Napoleon erected his first battery. The
next day it began to take effect, and the first serious attack
commenced. On the 18th and 19th the ships of the Allies
and this battery had a tremendous engagement. [2] On the
20th, the second battery was erected and "fired with more
effect on the ships"; "Gunboats suffered considerably and
the St. George had 21 men killed and wounded by the
bursting of one of her lower deck guns, the land batteries
were silenced before two o'clock, but altogether we had lost

---

[1] Lettre Salicetti, Sept. 26. R. A.
  Letter Mulgrave-Gazette.
[2] Hood's journal, September 18th.

about 70 men wounded or killed. Lord Hood became anxious about the shipping and that evening it was determined to occupy the heights of Grasse".[1] On September 20 the following was inserted in Lord Hood's journal. "The floating battery No. 1 hauled off, having received much damage." This is the official record of Napoleon's first hostile act against the British. On September 21st "Cannonade still in the northwest arm". "Mr. Gourly and people returned from the Floating battery No. 3, it being sunk by the Enemy's shot in the N. W. arm".

Napoleon's first batteries had been firing but a day or so when the possibility of being forced to leave the harbor was brought forcibly home to the two Admirals. The question immediately arose what was, in such a case, to be done with the French fleet. From now on this question remained a source of contention between the Admirals, and also between their respective courts. This difference had disastrous results and Napoleon's cleverly placed batteries were the cause of it. It was his first act that had any influence upon the events of his time, and it took place within the first few days of his arrival before Toulon. On October 3rd the Duke of Alcudia wrote to St. Helens. "As the case tho' remote may possibly occur in which the Spanish and English squadrons may be obliged to abandon the anchorage of Toulon from there being so much molested by bombs and red hot shells, as not to be able to remain there, His Majesty's pleasure upon this point has been signified to Admiral Langara by the Minister of Marine on the 1st instant, leaving, however, to the prudent discretion of the admiral, to settle and resolve in concert with Lord Hood whatever may according to existing circumstances, be found most advisable."[2] This is an official record of Napoleon's work during the first few days at Toulon. In the same letter the Spanish Minister proposed that in case it became necessary to leave the port, "Admiral

[1] Letter from Thomas Graham, September 25th. Life of Graham.
[2] St. Helens. R. O. Published by Cottin.

Langara shall sail, with all french ships that can be put to
sea to the islands of Hieres, or whatever other place he may
appoint in concert with Lord Hood, as most convenient,
carrying in them all the artillery, ammunition, arms and
stores which they can bring; leaving a manifest or protest
to the government of Toulon, if the latter should not
abandon the place that all ships of the french navy shall
be kept and taken care of, to be delivered, at a proper opportunity, to their lawful sovereign". "This instruction"
writes St. Helens "was prepared in consequence of the information that had been received from thence stating that
the enemy had succeeded in establishing a battery which in
some sort commanded the harbors and roads".[1] It will be
seen that the "manifest or protest" referred to by Alcudia
was apparently all that was to be left to the people of Toulon who had confided themselves to the English and Spaniards. Alcudia further proposed that such ships as could not
be removed should be sunk or set on fire. As this was later
on actually done, it will be seen how the Spanish regarded
their own proposal. (see part II). I do not mean to imply
in the least that the English were any more sincere in their
dealings with the people of Toulon or that they had any
more scruples in disposing of the French fleet. Hood wrote
to London that he used the French ships against the batteries thinking it better that they should be sunk than his
own.[2]

To prevent the enemy's batteries from being placed in a
still more dangerous position, on the heights of Grasse,
Admiral Gravina and Lord Mulgrave, the English commander landed at midnight Sept. 21st with about 500 men
at Balaguier, and gained the wooded heights above without
seeing any of the enemy. A post was established before day-
break on the most commanding point: in the afternoon it

---

[1] St. Helens to Grenville. Oct. 9th. R. O.
[2] Hood to Philip Stephens. Oct. 7. Admirals dispatches Mediterranean
1793. R. O.

was attacked by 600 men who approached under cover of
the wood. They were repulsed. The next day more troops
were sent out, woods were cut down in abatis, and the post
was well supplied with cannon. There were now 800 men
on the spot. Here the Allies gained a most deceided advantage; they had seized and fortified the most vulnerable
point surrounding Toulon, and the harbor. Napoleon on
his arrival had recognized the importance of this position
and went to Carteaux "pour lui offrir de le faire entrer dans
Toulon avant huit jours, s'il voulait faire occuper en force
la position du Caire (the Heights of Grasse) de manière que
l'artillerie put sur-le-champ placer des batteries à l'extremité des caps de l'Eguillette et de Balaguier".[1] Carteaux
whose favorite tactics were the use of the *arme blanc* failed
to see the importance of this position and allowed the allies
to proceed him.[2] Finally when he did make the attack, it
was done in such a half-spirited manner as to be easily
repulsed. Napoleon took no part in this attack, but on the
very same day his battery sunk one of the floating batteries
of the enemy. He as well as the Represantants du peuple
were loud in accusing Carteaux and lamenting his failure
to take the position. "Pourquoi ne l'avons-nous pas fait?
Parceque le général que nous avions cru comprendre et
adopter notre plan n'y avait aucune confiance quoique celui
que vous aviez envoyé de Paris fût exactement le même:
parce ceux qui l'entourent sont encore plus ignorants et
plus entétés que lui: parceque ni les uns, ni les autres n'ont
aucune connaissance ni des hommes qu'ils mênent ni des
machines militaires, ni de leurs effets: parce que toute
l'armée n'ayant trouvé jusqu'à présent aucune résistance
dans son expédition est toute découragée de celle que lui
presente Toulon—si l'absence de Carteaux (it was supposed
that he was going to the Army of Italy) nous donne un

[1] Memoires de Napoléon.

[2] Attack on Hauteurs de Grasse. Hood's Journal. Letter of Mulgrave
in Gazette. Letter from Graham, Life of Graham. Memoires and Correspondence of Napoleon. Salicetti to Comité Sept. 26 R. A.

général et des officiers supérieurs qui sentent mieux l'importance de la point des Vallons nous tenterons encore d'en chasser les Anglais".[1] Napoleon wrote on Nov. 14th to the Minister of War, referring to this attack:[2] "Dans ce moment là (while his batteries were fighting the enemy's ships) les ennemis comprenant l'insuffisance de leur artillerie navale risquèrent le tout pour le tout et débarquèrent à l'Eguillette; ils ussent dû être écrasé dans leur descent; la fatalité ou notre ineptie voulut qu'elle leur réûssît. Peu de jours après ils y eurent des pièces de 24, un chemin couvert et des palissades, quelques jours après, des secours considérables leur arrivèrent de Naples et d'Espagne. Je compris que l'affaire de Toulon était manquée et qu'il fallait se resoudre à un siege".

From here up to the first of October nothing of great importance happened. The fleet and land batteries continued an artillery duel; reinforcements arrived gradually for each side. Part of the French squadron was put in commission under the French Admiral Trogoff. Toulon was declared a free port and well supplied with provisions, chiefly from Spain and the Spanish islands. On Sept 23 the Republicans heard the fire of 21 guns from each ship of the fleet. It was in honor of the coronation of Louis XVII.[3]

On Oct. 1 Carteaux received the following note. "Les troupes de la Republique viennent d'enlever la montague du Faron, ses retranchements et sa redoute. Signé La Poype".[4] The commanding position of Faron was of great importance and La Poype decided to attack it. From the northern side it was considered inaccessible, except at Pas de la Masque, where one might reach the top by a narrow zigzag path; the English considered a strong post of sixty men sufficient to hold this pass. On the night of Sept. 30 La

---

[1] Lettre de Salicetti, Sept. 26th. R. A.
[2] Correspondance de Napoléon.
[3] Hood's Journal.
[4] Lettre de Salicetti. Oct. 1. R. O.

Poype formed his three attacking columns. The one on the right was to ascend the northwest end; it was under the command of Victor. La Poype commanded the center column, which was to attack at Pas de la Masque; the column on the left was to make a false attack. Victor led his column up the hill, along the ridge of the mountain eastward to Pas de la Masque; he drove the picket back into the redoute of Faron, assailed this on all sides at once, and cleared it out just as the enemy had run up their signal for help. While La Poypes triumphant note was on its way to Carteaux the alarming news of the taking of Faron reached the town. Reinforcements, of the best troops and in large numbers, as well as field pieces should have been hurried to Victor and his men. But this was not done. A few men did arrive before the end of the day, but they were such as did more harm than good. The ridge of Faron is formed by several heights running east and west. A deep ravine running northward from Toulon cuts deep into Mount Faron perpendicularly; it runs almost through to the northern side leaving only a narrow ridge connecting the heights on the east and west of this valley, which is called Valbourdin. On the south-western side of the ascent was Fort St. Antoine and on the south-eastern Fort Faron. The Allies, in contrast to the Republicans, showed the greatest activity and determination. At 7 o'clock the news reached the town: a council of war was held and the immediate attack determined upon. At 8 o'clock the troops started. English, Spanish Piedmontese and Neapolitans, good troops and of four nationalities, started forward to attack Victor and his small force. The result would not have been at all certain, had Victor been able to rely upon his troops; they were new, of inferior quality and such as are easily panic-stricken. Lord Mulgrave and Colonel de Revel lead the English and Piedmontese column up the south-west side of the mountain. On the most western ridge they met about 200 of the enemy, whom they drove back, aided by the guns of Fort St.

Antoine. The Republicans retreated eastward leaving a few prisoners in the hands of the English. As they discovered the Spanish column under Gravina, supported on the right by the Neapolitans who approached up the Valbourdin, they saw the possibility of their being cut off and quickened their march eastward. The English learned from the prisoners that the French, about 1500 strong were drawn up on the eastern end of Faron. They continued along the ridge to Valbourdin, and found Victor's force arranged in the form of a triangle one side facing west, the other south. The redoute of Faron lined with men, was in his rear, and between this redoute and his lines was placed the reserve. The valley Valbourdin widens off to the south-east in descending and thus protected Victor's left flank. Mulgrave got his men under cover before the narrow ridge, about 15 yards wide, which connects the height east and west of Valbourdin. To attack the French he had to cross this valley. It was decided to send Gravina, who had been approaching on the west side of Valbourdin, accross to the east to attack the left of the enemy. He turned off to the right, but in starting to cross he received a heavy fire from the French. This forced him to cross further down. The English waited for him to take up his position against the left of the enemy. This he did, following his advanced guard which was led by a Spanish sergeant who greatly distinguished himself. At first the left of Victor's force was exposed to a flank fire from the English and he moved part of it around to the right. As Gravina's column came up Victor's left had to be protected again and reinforced. When Gravina engaged it, it began to waver, and by doing so gave the English and Piedmontese the signal to advance over the narrow pass. This double attack by a superior force was too much for the French. They broke and retreated in the wildest disorder. The two attacking columns entered the redoute of Faron at the same moment. The French were persued and many of them were dashed to pieces in falling over the cliffs. The small English

force in Fort Faron seized this chance to fall upon the
flank of the retreating Frenchmen. Victor with the few
men he was able to keep around him, retreated in good
order. In spite of his defeat he was the hero of the day.
"Le chef de bataillon Victor, à qui on avait confié ce poste
s'est conduit à merveille et dans l'occupation et dans la
resistance qu'il a faite ; il a été nommé chef de brigade, une
voix unanime s'est levée pour lui." One of the English
officers wrote "A M. Victor is said to have been killed. He
was reckoned a good officer and all his dispositions that day
were in the style of a man who understood his business."
Victor distinguished himself later on during the siege.
The Republican loss on this day is very hard to give. The
Allies lost about 100 men. Gravina was wounded " in the
course of his able and spirited exertions at the head of the
Neapolitans grenadiers". All the troops fought well, writes
Mulgrave, " I should do injustice, should I particularize any
corps or any nation." The retaking of Mount Fafon was
very important to the Allies. " Hood was glad it was as it
gave an opportunity of recovering it so handsomely."[1]

This failure on the part of La Poype increased the ill-
feeling between him and Carteaux[2]. Carteaux relieved him
of his command. La Poype however was the brother-in-
law of Fréron, the Representant du peuple, and for this
reason he was soon reinstated. From now up to the end of
October the Republican army was in the most pitiable state[3];
there was jealousy between the commanding generals, and
ill-will between Carteaux and the Representants. On Oct.
12 Salicetti wrote "Carteaux a besoin, outre la bonne
volonté, des moyens personnels, et nous ne lui connaissons

[1] For the attack on Faron. Memoires de Thaon ; de Victor. Letters
from Graham. Mulgrave in Gazette. Letter from Hood, in Admirals'
Dispatches, Mediterranean 1793, R. O. Lettre de Gasparin et Salicetti
Oct. 4. R. A.

[2] Lettre Carteaux a La Poype. Oct. 3. A. G.

[3] Lettres de Ricord, Oct. 8 : de Salicetti, Oct. 10, 12, 23, 27 : de Freron-
Oct. 20. R. A.

pas d'autres que sa reputation." On Oct. 6th Carteaux wrote [1]
"Mais dites au Ministre, vous qui connaissez ma franchise
que si l'on croit quelqu'un plus capable que moi pour rem-
plir cette mission, que c'est avec reconnaissance que je céd-
erai un fardeaux que la trahison la plus noire m'a rendu
insupportable, car quel nom voulés vous que je donne à
une Phrase qui dit tout simplement que je l'eusse voulu les
Anglais ne seraient plus à Toulon et que peut penser de
moi le comité de Salut Public, à qui l'on fait entendre que
c'est pour avoir rejetté son plan que les Anglais ne sont
pas chassés."

The Republican soldiers were raw recruits, uncertain,
undisciplined and poorly armed; many of the troops who arrived had no arms at all.[2] Salicetti and Gasparin went themselves to Marseilles and with great difficulty obtained 3000
guns. The one redeeming feature of the Republican army
was the artillery.[3] Napoleon showed the greatest activity, col-
lecting cannon, powder, and material of every kind. He was
untiring in his efforts and definite in his purpose. His first
two batteries have already been spoken of. *La Montagne*
opened fire on Sept 18; *Les Sans Culottes*, on the the 20th.
"Située au bord de la mer à la pointe du Brégaillon; elle a
fait son effet, elle a chasssé tous les pontons, les bombardes
et les frégates qui se tenaient sur la gauche de l'Eguillette".
These two batteries cleared the petite rade north of L'Eguillette. The village La Seyne was thus protected. The next
battery, *Les Sablettes* was erected against Fort Mulgrave,
which continued to be Napoleon's object of attack. *Les
Sablettes* opened fire on Oct. 7

The Allies decided to attack it. They had learned from a

---

[1] Lettre de Carteaux à l'adjoint du Mtre de la Guerre, Archives de la
Guerre.

[2] Lettre de Veyrenne à Carteaux Oct. 6. Lettre de Carteaux au Min
istre de la Guerre. Oct. 7. Proclamation de Carteaux. Oct. 8. Archives
de la Guerre.

[3] Lettres de Carteaux. Sept. 29. Oct. 18. A. G. Lettre de Salicetti
Sept. 25. A. G.

deserter who knew the watchword, that it was defended by
troops of the last conscription. At half past two in the morning of Oct 9, 400 English and Spanish left Fort Mulgrave
to attack the battery. Led on by a French deserter, who
answered the sentinels, they entered the battery; the first
sentinel was killed, all who resisted were bayoneted. The
enemy was completely routed, after making a short stand.
They numbered about 300. The English spiked the guns,
sawed the gun-carriages and destroyed the ammunition
which was found in quantities At 4 o'clock they marched
back, having lost but 4 men killed and 7 wounded. The
Republicans lost 7 men killed and 10 wounded; also a few
prisoners among them 3 officers and the lieutenant of artillery who commanded the battery. The damage was not very
great. " A trois heures après midi la batterie se trouve parfaitement rétablie et en état de jour. Vous avez ci. joint des
proclamations que les enemis ont laissées eu profusion en
abandonnant la batterie. nos soldats ne croient pas au ten-
dre intérêt des puissances coalisées pour la dynastie que
nous avons culbuté due trone. "

[1] Napoleon's activity continued, new batteries were constantly being erected. Hood's record for these days is full
of " heavy cannonading between the ships and batteries."
" The enemy's gun and mortar Batteries are constantly
playing upon our posts and shipping without our having
the means of driving them to a greater distance."[2] At this
time the Allied forces amounted to about twice the number
of the besieging army: their troops were undoubtedly better.
Why they did not make some successful sallies is hard to
explain. In the meantime however the number of con-
scripts raised in the Var amounted to about 13,000 young
men; and fresh battalions arrived daily. Were they all

[1] Attack of Sablettes. Gasparin. Oct 7. R. A. Memoires de Napoléon
Mulgrave in Gazette. Hood in Gazette.

[2] Letter from Hood to John Trevor. Public Record Office. Foreign
Office. Sardinia. 1793. Oct to Dec. Letters from Trevor to Grenville.

armed, it would perhaps have been possible to have made an attack one of the posts. As it was, the artillery was the only arm which annoyed the Allies in the least. The Petite Rade was gradually cleared of the ships, which were taken back to a safer position.

On Oct. 13th. news arrived of the fall of Lyons. The besieging army celebrated it in true republican style. Extra rations of *eau-de-vie* were distributed. There was dancing, music and singing. Whole battalions danced around in rings. The news was announced to the town by the shot and shell from a new battery which Napoleon had just completed : *Bréguart*, about 300 yards south of *Les Sablettes* "elle balaye les rives de la droite de l'Eguillette et toute cette partie de la Grande Rade."[1] The Allies decided to stop this rejoicing and the next day, they made a sortie. Thaon de Revel termed it "une étourdie militaire". At 11 o'clock in the morning 3000 of the Allies took up a defensive position behind the Riviere Neuve. 100 men were sent out to Hauteur des Arennes to discover the movements of the enemy. A patrol of 800 men was sent out on the left. These advance bodies got too far forward and in protecting their retreat a general action came on. The Allies retired to their position, and awaited the attack of the Republicans, but as night came on they retired to Fort Malbousquet. In giving an account of this engagement Carteaux praised Almeras highly. [2]"L'intelligence et les talents du citoyen Almeras ont forcé nos ennemis à se reployer". He did not mention Bonaparte, nor can I find anywhere a justification for Chuquet's saying that he led the troops on this day. [3]Carteaux praised the work of the batteries in the same letter, however "Tant qu'à nos Batteries elles font le meilleur effet possible surtout la batterie des Sans-culottes . . . elle coupe de temps en temps quelques mats et maltraite les fréegates".

---

[1] Correspondance de Napoleon.
[2] " Carteaux au M. de la Guerre, Oct. 18, A. G.
[3] Chuquet—page 188.

The next day, October 15, it was the Republican's turn to take the offensive. Lapòype made an attack on Cap Brun,[1] but after a stubborn fight was driven back. The post was supposed to be in safety, but before long a second and much stronger column advanced, covered by the artillery. This time the Allies were soon driven from the post; four English officers fell in defending it. Once more a hurried Council of War was held at Toulon on the news of the loss of the post. "On délibéra à Toulon si l'on attaquerait le Cap Brun de vive force, ou si l'on obligerait l'ennemi à l'évacuer par un mouvement qui menaca de les envelopper". It was decided to outflank the Republicans. The position of the enemy was reconnoitred and it was found that they had abandoned Cap Brun, forming their whole line on a height further to the east, their left covered by Castle Ste Marguerite, which had two twelve pounders turned toward the land. Field pieces could be seen well distributed along the front of the enemy's line. The Allies marched under the protection of the guns of Fort Faron to La Vallette, leaving behind them 140 men with two 18 pounders, who with the guns from Fort Faron were to block the Vallon Favières and prevent the enemy from sending reinforcements by this pass from their post at Tourris and Revest. From La Vallette, they started for the Hauteurs de Thouars, a position commanding La Garde, and which would have given the allies control of the entire plain and of all the roads to the east of Toulon. From this position the Republicans might have been forced miles away from the east side of the city. The Republicans saw their danger and moved in all haste from their position toward La Garde. Owing to the mistake of the guide, and to the rather slow manœuvres of the Spanish and Neapolitan infantry which headed the column, the Republicans reached La Garde at the same time as the Allies gained the heights of Thouars. The battle now resolved itself into a heavy cannonade from each side. "Les Français firent un

---

[1] Attack on Cap Brun. Thaon. Elphinstone in Gazette.

mouvement comme pour couper aux alliés le chemin de
Toulon mais leur cavalerie mise en désordre par le canon,
se retire bientôt. Les dragons de la Reine espagnole manœuv-
rirent avec audace et succès". 160 of these cavalrymen
had just arrived three days before. When night came on
the noise of the artillery and wagons leaving La Garde was
distinctly heard, and as the Republicans did not answer the
heavy guns of the allies, it was supposed that they had
evacuated the place. A few men were sent ahead "pour s'en
assurer, mais le feu violent qui en partit, fit connaître qu'il
était encore occupé". The object of the allies had been ac-
complished and they returned to Toulon. This was the only
fight around Toulon of skillful manœuvring where all three
arms were employed.

The operations dragged on slowly, but the outlook for the
Republicans was not bright. Fréron and Barras wrote from
Marseilles: "A present les ennemis se sont renforcés et se
renforcent tous les jours. Carteaux n'a aucune des connais-
sances militaires propres à s'emparer d'une des places les
mieux fortifiées de la Republique"—Reinforcements were
looked for from Toulon. In these days of depression Bonaparte was the only one who was active. On October 18th he
opened a new battery, Des 4 Moulins, située à 700 toises de
la redoute anglaise."[1] For the same day, can be read in
Hood's Journal: "A heavy fire commenced from Hauteur
de Grasse and ships in the N. W. Arm." The garrison of Fort
Mulgrave began to see the danger of their position. For
three days they kept up a continual fire on Napoleon's batteries, but failed to destroy any of them. And on October 22
they were attacked by still another; La Grande Rade, "elle
fait le même effet que celle du Bréguart". Hood's attention
was continually called to Fort Mulgrave. On October 23 he
wrote in his Journal; "Made the General signal to assist
Camel with boats". This short sentence is proof that the
Camel approached too close to Bonaparte's battery. About

---

[1] Correspondance de Napoleon.

this time the powder became rather scarce and the batteries were not so noisy. In the meantime Napoleon was busily employed on four or five new ones; all in different stages of completion.

The constant yet somewhat unjust complaints against Carteaux had at last taken effect, and on October 21 he received notice that he was to be replaced at Toulon by General Doppet, who had commanded at Lyons. From now on until the departure of Carteaux on November 7 the siege rather dragged, although the monotony was broken now and then by a day of "heavy cannonading", as it was termed in Hood's Journal. No great harm seems to have been done. On October 30th the Terrible "signalled for assistance," but in general the ships keep at a safe distance. The last week in October troops and cannon began to arrive from Lyons and Grenoble, as well as many troops from the new levies; for the Representants were quite busy dispatching raw and useless recruits to the walls of Toulon.[1] On October 25 Salicetti and Gasparin received news from Doppet informing them that he had sent off 3,000 troops. As they had expected 20,000 this information gave them a good deal of alarm, which they quickly made known to the Comité de Salut public. The Allies also received reinforcements, which added to the discouragement of the Republicans. Discipline in the Republican army was still bad and desertion frequent. At last on November 5 some good troops arrived from Lyons. Two days afterwards Carteaux left, complaining bitterly against Doppet "qui n'a point de talents militaires," [2] and against Lapoype "qui s'est conduit de manière à faire soupçonner sa fidelité" [2] He accused even the Representants; something which was very dangerous to do in that day. "Quel rôle me fait-on jouer? Les forces de Lyons devoient sans retard marcher sur Toulon. il semble

---

[1] Letters under date of November 2. A. G.
    Letters from Oct. 22 to Nov. 5 from Representants. R. A.
[2] Lettre de Carteaux au Ministre de la Guerre. Nov. 5th. A. G.

qu'une main les retienne et je suis obligé de surveiller jour et nuit une troupe fatigué de trois mois de Bivouac, et lorsque les moyens d'agir avec efficacité arriveront ceux qui m'ont liés les bras viendront pour que je leur cède la place, ils se sont bien gardés de hater les secours—ils n'ont écouté que leur ambition et la chose publique ne pouvant être sauvé par eux, ils n'ont pas voulu qu'un brave homme la sauve ".[1] Carteaux was quite right in saying that he was being removed just at the moment when things were taking a brighter turn.[2]

On Nov 5th. the Minister of War sent word to Doppet that he was to go to the Pyrenees : Cartèaux was to be put in command of the Army of the Alpes to hold the Piedmontese in check : and General Dugommier was to take command at Toulon. [3] Doppet did not arrive until the 13th. From the 6th until this time Lapoype held the command. The real head of the army however was Salicetti, with whom at this time Napoleon had the greatest influence. He therefore practically had his hands free and if he felt that he was himself capable of directing an attack on Toulon he might through the influence of Salicetti attempt it ; in spite of the fact that Doppet had given Lapoype instructions to remain on the defensive. [4]It seems in reality as if such an attack was made altho it is impossible to get positive proof of it. The following is found in Pon's Memoires. It is said to have happened on Nov. 9 ; " La matinée l'ennemi attaquait le camp Balaguier mais sans succes. L'après-midi il feignait de marcher sur Malbousquet et Saint-Antoine dans le temps que le Général Lapoype simulait une attaque contre le Cap Brun. puis tout à coup se porta de nouveau sur Belaguier avec 12 à 1500 hommes et fit encore une fois contraint de se retirer. Il revint à la charge ver les sept heures du soir avec 2 ṿ 3000 hommes. Le camp menacé venait de recevoir

---

[1] Lettre de Carteaux à l'Adjoint au Ministre de la Guerre. Nov. 4. A.

[2] Lettre de Salicetti. Nov 9. R. A.

[3] Mtre. de la Guerre au Gen. Doppet. Nov. 5. A. G.

[4] Lettre Salicetti. Nov. 9. R. A.

des troupes fraîches et des munitions. On laissa les republicans s'approcher des retranchements et au moment ou ils croyaient se rendre maîtres un feu très vif de mousqueterie et une décharge à mitraille de l'artillerie les forcèrent à abandonner précipitamment le champ de bataille qui resta couvert de morts et de blessés ". This is rather a circumstantial account and is strengthened by the following which Salicetti wrote on Nov. 9th.[1] " Il nous arrive enfin des munitions, des pieces d'artillerie de l'armée de Lyon. . . . nous sommes maîtres d'une position où nous sommes occuper à nous fortifier, d'où nous pourrons incendier les édefices de l'infame Toulon, en les designant au doigt . . . on se prépare à attaquer les ennemis en même temps dans la rade, dans la ville et dans plusieurs forts ". In other words Salicetti said they had just received more munitions and artillery, that they occupied a strong position; (he must have referred to the heighs upon which the Battery, the Convention, was situated, and that they were planing the very kind of an attack which according to Pons was made. In Hood's Journal— Nov 9. "Terrible made signal for assistance. made Royal and Robust signals for their boats to go to the assistance of the Terrible". Here at least is proof that the attack upon the Rade was made. It seems quite probable that this was the work of Bonaparte who had induced Salicetti to risk an attack. As Lopoype and probably all the officers were involved in it; as it was a failure; and as it was carried out against orders, it is not surprising that there should be no official account of it. The affairs of the Republican Army were carried on in such a loose manner, that even such an attack might be passed over without being noticed. The attack was, according to Pons' description, a spirited one, but it proved somewhat premature and at all events a failure. During this period before the arrival of Doppet, Napoleon had been especially active in the erection of batteries: the material for these was furnished by

---

[1] Recueil Aulard.

Lyons and Grenoble. On Nov. 9th. Salicetti wrote "On terminera la nuit prochaine une batterie qui produira dans la Grande Rade le même effet que les Sans-Culottes dans la Petite". Nov 12.[1] "le 22 au 23 Brumaire la batterie des Sablettes a fait une feu terrible sur la redoute des Anglais, a fait sauter un magazin à poudre et tué beaucoup de monde par l'eclat des bombes qui ont pris feu. Demain une nouvelle batterie, dite les hommes-sans-peur fera feu sur la Batterie ennemi. une autre dite la convention nationale battera Malbousquet". Nov 13th [2]"On travaille avec ardeur à la construction de nouvelles batteries. A l'arrivée du général nous ésperons de frapper de grands coups et d'avoir des nouvelles importantes à vous communiquer". Hood wrote on Nov 13th. [3]"their batteries approach by degrees both toward the town and the fleet and it is of the highest importance that the garrison should be made strong enough to go out and destroy their works". As is seen, by the arrival of Doppet Bonaparte's branch of the army had made the greatest progress : Napoleon had selected the position of, and started to erect, every battery which was used up to the fall of Toulon.[4] Therefore to him and to him alone belongs the credit of the principal arm of the besieging army at Toulon.

Doppet arrived on November 13th. He saw at once that he did not possess the necessary qualifications for carrying on a seige such as that of Toulon and [5]consented to stay only if it would be under the orders of Dugommier. Luck would have it however that the few days in which he was in command were rather exciting ones.

On November 15 an engagement took place. The following is Napoleon's account of it. [6]The soldiers of the battalion

---

[1] Lettre Salicetti. Nov 12th. Archives de la Guerre. (Not published in Recueil Aulard.)

[2] Lettre Salicetti. R. A.

[3] Letter to John Trevor. Record Office. Sardinia.

[4] Letter Nov 14th. Correspondance de Napoleon. Here the future position of every battery afterwards erected is mentioned.

[5] Salicetti. November 17th. R. A.

[6] Memoires de Napoléon.

Côte d' Or stationed opposite Fort Mulgrave, seeing the Spaniards ill-treat a French prisoner, seize their arms and rush to his assistance. Other battalions follow and soon a whole division is engaged. Doppet and Bonaparte rush to the Scene. "Le vin est tiré, il faut le boire" says Napoleon in advising Doppet rather to continue the action than to withdraw the troops. Doppet allows him to direct the attack. Bonaparte places himself at the head of the tirailleurs who cover the hill, and forming two columns tries to penetrate into the Fort at its gorge. O'Hara, the Governor of Toulon, sees the action and hastens to Fort Mulgrave to urge on his troops, he makes a sortie which is vigorously supported by a cannonade from the ships and Fort. Doppet, seeing one of his aids killed at his side, gives the signal for retreat. Napoleon is furious and galloping toward Doppet exclaims, "Toulon est manqué, et un . j . f . . . . a fait battre la retraite." Such is Napoleon's account which Cottin [1] puts aside, and then relates how it was "en réalité." In the War Archives a contempory and detailed report of this engagement exists and I shall give it about in full. It will be seen that it is quite reconcilable with Napoleon's account.

[2] "Rapport du Citoyen Brulé, Chef du 2[le] Bon de la Côte d'Or, commandant la division ditte de la Plaine à l'armée Revolutionnaire près Toulon.

---

[1] Cottin. page 266.

[2] Cottin's authorities are Thaon de Revel: Boullement de Lachenaye. Journal de Vernes. Raports Napolitains. (He admits that the Journal de Vernes is inexact: Thaon de Revel's account does not conflict with Napoleon's: I found the Raports Napolitains in London, but put them aside as scanty and containing nothing of value). With these Cottin relates how it was "en réalité." Napoleon's account is corroberated by the report of Brulé, the account of Doppet (letter Nov 17th. Archives de la Guerre) and a letter from O'Hara under date of Nov 15th. in the Gazette. Attacks on this day were frequent. Doppet writes, "L'ennemi voyant commencer des travaux trop près de lui et s'élever des batteries qui rendroient la prise des siennes moines difficiles a pris le parti de faire à chaque instant des sorties du côté de nos travailleurs " . . . "Le même jour (15th Nov.) nous avons été attaqué à notre droite du côté des Sablettes au centre du côté de Malbousquet, et à la gauche du côté du fort St. Antoine. non contentes de les repousser, nos troupes ont à la gauche et à la droite poursuivi l'ennemi jusque dans ses retranchements. cependant cette affaire étant générale n'ayant eu ni donné aucune plan d'at-

Le 25e jour du 2° Mois de la de année 2 de la Republique française une patrouille ennemie s'étant présentée devant la Seine nos postes avancées furent à sa rencontre. Le combat s'engage entre elles. Ces patrouilles se grossirent de Part et d'autre de manière qu'au bout de trois quarts d'heures on eut dît que c'était deux armées au lieu de Patrouilles. Moi sousigné m'étant transporté sur les lieux je ralliai les troupes de la Republique et ordonnai la charge. Alors nos troupes fondèrent sur l'ennemi avec un tel acharnement que je ne pus les empecher d'aller jusqu'a la redoute ennemie. M'y étant transporté moi-même je jugeai qu'il aurait été imprudent de tenter un assaut puisque ce poste ne nous aurait été d'aucune utilité pour le moment attendu l'impossibilité de pouvoir le conserver. En consequence je ordonnai la retraite qui s'effectua dans le meilleur ordre possible. Nous avons perdus dans cette affaire qu'a duré 5 heures 10 à 12 hommes qui sont morts sur le champ de bataille et environ 15 blessés. . . . L'ennemi a eu environ 60 ou 70 hommes tués dont la pluspart ont été tués dont leur redoute, nous leur avons fait aussi un prisonnier." Here the chief of the Battalion Cote d'Or admits that his men got away from him, and it is quite possible that while he was sounding the retreat, Napoleon was trying to form the scattered, but still advancing troops into column to enter the fort. It is also not surprising that Napoleon thought Doppet had given orders to sound the retreat; which he may also have done.

---

taque, les forces étant de plus trop divisées pour en esperer en avançant des avantages reels et durables chaque chef de colonne fit engager ses postes à sa troupe ". This shows that Doppet had no plan of attack, that each *chef* directed his own affair, and that regarding the engagements in such a light, it is quite possible that Doppet sounded the retreat when he found his soldiers too far advanced. Cottin says the "l'objectif réel des republicains était toujours Balaguier, contre lequel Doppet lança d'abord 50, puis 500, enfin 1500 hommes ". The attack on Balaguier was the all important one, but it was not Doppet who directed it, nor were the other attacks false ones, made by Doppet, as Cottin puts it. Napoleon took part in the attack of Balaguier, and nothing can be found to disprove his account of it.

O'Hara writes, " Mulgrave vigorously and repeatedly attacked by a large corps of the enemy."

CHAPTER III.

Dugommier—Marescot—Council of War—Bonaparte's
Plan—Marescot's influence upon the Siege—At-
tack on Convention—Artillery before Final At-
tack—Attack on Eguillette—Council of War—
Departure of Allies—Destruction of the ships—
Entrance of Republicans—Bonaparte and the
Massacres.

On Nov. 17 Dugommier arrived. He was far a better general than Carteaux, Lapoype, or Doppet. Fifty-five years
old, he had seen some service. He was formally an officer
in a marine battery; he took part with some distinction in
the Seven Years War, and also in the American War of
Independence. Then he retired to his estate in the West
Indies, from whence he had been sent as a deputy to Paris;
later he re-entered the army, was made brigadier general in
Oct. 1792. In the Italian army he likewise distinguished
himself, became general of division: in short he was a good
soldier.

An old artillery general, Du Theil, arrived two hours
after Dugommier. Doppet and Albitte had brought him to
take charge of the artillery, but he was forced to remain a
few days in Marseilles, and consequently did not arrive with
Doppet. About this time a decided and continual improve-
ment took place in the condition of the besieging army.
Reinforcements, artillery and ammunition arrived in great
quantity: these came principally from Lyons. The taking
of this city had a great effect upon the attack of Toulon, as
it permitted about all the forces employed there to be turned
against the Allies in Toulon. There was however difficulty
in finding provisions for the Republican army, and toward
the end of the siege this question became one of great importance.[1]

On Nov. 24 the chef de bataillon, Marescot, a friend of
Carnot's arrived, " pour diriger le génie ". The next day he

---

[1] Lettres de Salicetti. Nov. 9 to 13. R. A.

wrote to Carnot; " J'ai été visiter les attaques qui ne sont autre chose que quelques batteries provisoires dressées par les officiers d'artillerie destinées à combattre les batteries avancées des rebelles et à favoriser les premières opérations qui doivent avoir lieu le plus tôt possible ".[1] This was his first impression, a little later he wrote somewhat differently. On Jan 9th. 1794 in a Relation de la prise de Toulon he wrote "nos dispositions d'attaque n'étaient autre chose que des batteries provisoires placées avantageucement par le chef de bataillon Bonaparte, commandant en second de l'artillerie ".[2] Here he admitted that the batteries were placed "avantageusement" and by Bonaparte. His terming them " batteries provisoires" was quite wrong; he probably meant that in their construction they had not all the complete details such as would appeal to the eyes of an engineer. This was the case, but under the circumstances (dirth of workmen etc.) was quite unavoidable. It will be seen what success the engineers had in trying to complete these batteries. Their positions were their strong points and, as it has been seen, the course of the siege proved this to Marescott.

On Nov 25th. Dugommier held a council of war: the Representants, the generals, Bonaparte, Marescot and others were present There has been a good deal written about the plan of attack followed at Toulon; attempts made to prove that Napoleon was its originator, as well as to prove the contrary; yet no one seems to have laid stress upon the fact that on Nov 14, therefore 10 days before the council of war, Bonaparte in a letter to the Minister of War,[3] proposed a plan of attack which corresponded in almost every detail with that decided upon in the Council: As Napoleon drew up the *procès verbal* of the council, both the plans are published in his Correspondance. The war council decided: to make the principal attack on Eguillette:[4] to attack Mal-

---

1 Letter from Marescot. Nov 25th. R. A.

2 Relation de la prise de Toulon, écrit le 9 Janvier 1794. par le Général Marescot, Archives de la Guerre.

3 Correspondance de Napoléon.

4 Lettre 25 Novembre. Correspondance de Napoléon.

bousquet with the batteries la Convention and la Poudrière, so to deceive the enemy as to the point of attack, and to prepare the way for the infantry "si les evenements en permettent l'attaque": to establish a battery against Cap Brun to deceive the enemy as to the point of attack; to take Faron: all attacks were to be made at the same time: the "division de droite" was to attack Eguillette and to make a false attack on Malbousquet (this "false" attack was to be carried out if possible) the "division de gauche" was to make the attack on Faron and a false attack on Cap Brun. Much of the plan related to the batteries. It was decided; to erect batteries "à l'extremité du promontoire de l'Eguillette, afin d'obliger l'escadre à évacuer la rade et même de la brûler, si un vent contraire s'oppose à sa sortie": to erect one against Cap Brun; another "de 6 mortiers à grande portée contre Toulon" between la Convention and Malbousquet: to establish a " redoute de protection sur la gauche de la montagne de la Convention pour empêcher que l'ennemi favorisé par le feu des redoutes de Sainte Antoine ne tourne et n'elève la batterie de la Convention". Napoleon wrote in his above mentioned letter of Nov 14th. "Chasser les ennemis de la rade est le point préliminaire . . . . pour se rendre maître de la rade il faut se rendre maître de la pointe de l'Eguillette. Au même moment que nous serions maîtres de la pointe de l'Eguillette, il faudrait bombarder Toulon avec 8 ou 10 mortiers. Nous sommes maîtres de la hauteur des Arènes qui n'en est pas à 900 toises et nous pourrons facilement nous approcher à 800 toises sans passer la rivière neuve: dans le même temps l'on placerait deux batteries devant le fort Malbousquet, et une contre le fort l'Artigues. . . . Aujourd'hui il serait possible que quoique la flotte fut obligé d'évacuer la rade la garnison tînt encore et soutînt le siège. Alors les 2 batteries que nous aurions établis contre Malbousquet seraient promptement renforcées par une troisième: les mortiers qui pendant 3 jours auraient bombardé Toulon se tourneraient pour ruiner les défenses

de Malbousquet. Le fort ne résistera pas 48 heures et rien ne nous arrête alors jusqu'au front de Toulon. Nous attaquons le front composé par le bastion du Marais et le bastion de l'arsenal par une attaque brusquée qui nous conduit tout de suite à la deuxième parallèle favorisés par les batteries placées au Malbousquet et par celles placées sur le revers des Arénes. Nous serions gênés dans cette opération par le fort l'Artigues mais 4 mortiers et les 6 pièces de canon qui y aurait été placés au premier moment de l'attaque, y resteraient et feraient alors un feu plus vif" . . . . . Then he continued " La prise de l'Eguillette, l'expulsion des Anglais des rades et le bombardement et dans le même temps attaquer le Faron". From carefully comparing these two plans, it will be seen that Napoleon's was practically the same as the one decided upon in the council of war. Napoleon did not speak of the false attack against Cap Brun, and proposed batteries to be erected against Fort Artigues and not against the redoute Sainte Antoine, as it is mentioned in the final plan. With these two exceptions they are about identical. This shows conclusively that Napoleon was quite decided as to the proper plan of attack before the arrival of Dugommier. It is wrong however to say that Bonaparte was the sole originator of this plan, or to attribute any great merit to him if he had been. There were at least three vital points around Toulon; the most vital was certainly Fort La Malgue; this the Republicans could not well attack as it was strong for two reasons: the English had first landed there, and used it as a point of protection for their fleet; again all the Forts on the east side of Toulon had been better built, as it was from the east that any possible land attack on Toulon was supposed to come. Faron was also a position of great importance. This had been recognized at once by the Republicans, but their attack upon it had failed in the end. Lastly the Eguillette: this was also a splendid point of attack and the easiest to approach. Napoleon had recognized this immediately; but any well instructed officer would have done so. That Carteaux, who understood nothing about the use of artillery and whose tactics consisted in using the Bayonette, had not seen this, is not so surprising.

Someone had however sent this advice, the attacking of Eguillette, from Paris. Salicetti wrote on Sept 26th. to the Comité du Salut Public, [1] accusing Carteaux for having allowed the English to get possession of Eguillette. "Le général que nous avions cru comprendre et adopter notre plan n'y avait aucune confiance quoique celui que vous avez envoyé de Paris fût exactement le même". On Sept 25th. he wrote to the Minister of War. "Nous l'aurions forcé de quitter la rade, si ce général avait voulu executer le plan que nous lui avons proposé et qui etait celui du comité de Salut Public".[2] The idea of attacking the Eguillette came therefore from Paris. Bonaparte, as was natural had seen that it was the best point to attack and his batteries were erected against it, and did the greatest part toward taking it. The Republican Army had however, after the council of war, a plan which was agreed upon by all; it was no longer Bonaparte's idea only. Every one went to work to carry it out. The condition of the army was however far from satisfactory in many ways. Barras wrote from Marseilles on Nov 19th. "La situation de l'armée n'est pas satisfaisant" Victor said in his Memoires "Notre armée était jeune, pleine d'ardeur, mais il n'était point facile de la soumettre aux lois d'une exacte discipline". Marescot le chef du génie, had the greatest difficulty in trying to carry out his elaborate plans of a "siège en règle". The workmen were wanting, implements were hard to obtain, and he met with little encouragement on all sides. Finally however he became convinced that one must proceed in the most practical manner, and get along without that which it was impossible to obtain: but when at last, he was convinced of this fact the siege was about over; consequently Marescot,

---

[1] Recueil Aulard.
[2] Archives de la Guerre.

even as chef du génie, had no influence upon the direction
of the siege. Dec 10 he wrote "je vois que chacun ici est
persuadé qu'il ne sera pas nécessaire de devellopper des
attaques réguliéres pour reduire Toulon, j' aime à le croire
et même je le presume"; and after frequent complaints to
his friend Carnot of the insufficiency of the material necessary for his branch of the army he ended by admitting that
up to Dec. 10 he had done nothing.[1] Those who strive to
deminish the role of Bonaparte at Toulon lay stress upon
the fact that Marescot arrived at the same time as Dugommier; and to direct the siege.

One branch of the army continually and regularly increased, and that was the artillery. From now on to the end
it will be seen how the Republican artillery kept up a constant and effective fire upon the entire western side of
Toulon, until the Allied fleet sailed from the harbor in
haste. Nelson wrote on Dec 1st.[2] "shot and shells are very
plentiful all over the harbor. I wonder more damage has
not yet been done". General O'Hara I hope will be able
to drive the French from the heights near the harbour or
we shall be unpleasantly situated, not that I think Toulon
is in the slightest danger. At all events we can destroy the
French fleet and Arsenal in a very short time".

On Nov 28th the battery La Convention was opened
upon Fort Malbousquet; it apparently did no very great
damage; but its commanding position worried the Allies a
great deal, and it was decided to make a sortie and try to
destroy it.[3] About 3000 troops, British, Spanish, Neapolitan Piedmontese and French refugies left the garrison about

---

[1] Marescot à Carnot. Dec. 10th. Archives de la Guerre.

[2] Nelson's Dispatches.

[3] Attack on Convention.

Lettre du Général Garnier. Nov 30th. Archives de la Guerre.

Lettre de Salicetti. Nov. 30th. Letter from Elliot.

Thaon. Letter to Sir W. Hamilton, Correspondence. British Museum Mss. Egerton 2638.

Relation de Marescot. Lettre de Dugommier, Archives Nationales A. F. 1,281. Letters from Hood and Dundas in Gazette.

four in the morning, and supported by field artillery and
the guns of Malbousquet, marched upon the Hauteur des
Arènes. The Republicans were taken more or less by surprise and driven back in great confusion. The Allies however instead of forming on the height and preparing
themselves for a counter attack which was certain to come,
pursued the French along the road towards Ollioules, or
stopped to plunder. Even the spiking of the guns was carried out slowly and imperfectly. The news of the success of
the Allies was soon spread through tho camp. General Garnier, who commanded in this division, was making a stubborn retreat with the few reliable men which he could
gather around him, when Dugommier, Bonaparte and others
soon came on the scene with reinforcements. The Allies
were attacked with decision by superior forces, in the flank,
and at a moment when they were in confusion. Threatened
to be cut off from the town they retreated in great haste
and disorder, the Republicans following close on their heels.
The Piedmontese went back in less disorder than the others,and
they were also about the only ones prepared to make a stand
on the Heights: alone, however, they could do nothing. The
Allies brought their field pieces back from the Rivière Neuve
with great difficulty, as the Republicans followed them so
closely, and with such determination right up to the works
of Malbousquet, which they tried to enter by repeated attacks. The guns of this fort and those of the Redoute Ste.
Antoine forced them to retire. " Le combat a été bien
chaude " wrote Salicetti; and Napoleon " La matiné a été
belle ". The fight was clearly to the advantage of the Republicans, as the Convention and three other batteries were
blazing away harder than ever in a day or so; and the
Allies in their attempt lost about 700 of their best troops
killed, wounded, or taken prisoners: among the latter was
General O'Hara and about 17 officers. O'Hara was at first
with the reserve on the Riviére Neuve, but after the Allies
had taken the Convention, he advanced for some unknown

reason to the battery, received a wound in the arm and as the Allies fell back he was left behind and a few Republican soldiers from the bataillon d'Isère made him prisoner. It was not only around the Hauteur des Arènes but on the entire western side that the fight took place. The Republican batteries hurled shot at Fort Mulgrave and at the fleet, both of which answered in the most spirited manner. The artillery played an important part in driving the Allies back from the Convention, as well as in protecting Garnier's retreat at the beginning of the engagement. Just what part Napoleon took in this affair is hard to say, as accounts are so conflicting. But at all events there is absolute proof that he distinguished himself. [1] " Parmi ceux qui se sont le plus distingués et qui m'ont le plus aidé à rallier et à pousser en avant, ce sont le citoyens Buonaparte commandant l'artillerie, Arèna et Cervoni, adjudants généraux ". Salicetti wrote on this day, " Le général Mouret, Garnier et Buonaparte se sont dans cette occasion conduits d'une manière distinguée ".[2] It will be noticed that he was mentioned by Dugomier first among those who aided him, and that by Salicetti he was mentioned with two of the generals, and lastly, that he is the only one who is named in both reports.

The next two weeks were spent in preparing the batteries and in frequent artillery duels. This arm had at last assumed most formidable proportions [3], thanks to the activity of Bonaparte in procuring material of every description from Marseilles, Lyons, Grenoble, Biancon, etc., and to his judgement in selecting the positions of his batteries. Victor wrote that by Dec. 6. 194 bouches à feu were turned against Toulon; " or ces puissants moyens étaient dirigés par Bonaparte; car le Général Dutheil émervillé de la justesse et de la supériorité de ses vues s'était complétement effacé devant lui ". [4] Some idea of the amount of work required in the artillery

[1] Lettre de Dugommier. Nov. 30. Archives de la Guerre.

[2] Lettre de Salicetti Nov. 30 R. A.

[3] Letter from O'Hara. Archives Nationales AF II 9.

[4] Memoires de Victor.

may be gathered frim the following report of Dutheil to the Minister of War, on December 2nd. [1] " Personnel de l'artillerie—il faudrait 6 officiers superieurs, autants d'adjutants majors, un directeur du Parc, un sous directeur, un commissaire des guerres un proposé du payeur 'general, 20 conducteurs des charrios il n'y a pas le quart de cannoniers necessaires. . . . il faudrait au moins 8 commissaires de plus. Les cannoniers auxiliaires n'ayant que de la valeur et aucune instruction. . . . Poudre de la Guerre—Gassendi chef de Bataillon envoyé par les representans du peuple dans toutes les places jusqu'à Metz et Strasbourg pour notre approvisionnement de siège anonce que c'est la partie qui nous manquera le plus, quelque soit ses efforts pour nous en procurer - - -" The question of infantry cartridges was a most vital one. Bonaparte, and later Duteuil were loud in denouncing the wasteful expenditure here, especially in the affair of November 30. At last Salicetti took most severe measures for stopping this. Even as late as December 10 Dugommier wrote to the Minister of War " La poudre et les autres munitions de guerre exigent encore ta sollicitude. Je t'ai mandé que nous étions bien loin de la quantité calculée raisonablement et nécessaire à notre but." A day or so before the attack of the Convention three new batteries were opened. The *Convention ;* the *Homme-sans-peur,* " située sur un mamelon dominé par le camp anglais (Fort Mulgrave) Le général en a arrêté la construction par ce qu'il croyait l'infanterie trop faible pour s'y soutenir". ; and the *Petite Rade,* destinée à éloigner les bâtiments de la côte et des voisinages de la poudrière ".[2] On December 1 the Poudrière opened fire on Malbousquet. " Observed a great deal of cannonading and musketry at the different Posts & more especially near Fort Malbousquet ", Such was the account of it in Hood's Journal.

Dugommier became more and more enthusiastic over the

---

[1] Archives de la guerre.
[2] Correspondance de Napoleon.

artillery. On November 30 he wrote to the Minister of War "J'attends la perfection de deux batteries qui doivent jouer un beau role dans cette journée".[1] Dec. 4, "Les batteries necessaires à l'execution du dernier plan sont presque entierement achevées – – – Nous sommes pauvres en artilleurs." Dec. 10—"Chaque jour notre position s'ameliore par la perfection des batteries necessaires à l'attaque des postes exterieures qu'occupe l'ennemi et indiqués dans mon plan d'attaque. Je voudrais pouvoir t'en dire autant des autres moyens qui doivent contribuer à nos succes." About this time the batteries *La Farinière*, to the right of the *Convention*, and *Jacobins* to the left of *Hommes-sans-Peur*, and directed against Fort Mulgrave, were opened on the enemy. On Dec. 13, Lord Hood wrote that there was nothing of importance since the 30th of November, but that new batteries were going up on all sides, and that two of them " did us some mischief, on the 9th and 10th." " We shall soon have more men in the hospital than are fit for service".[2] Dundas wrote on December 12 "The enemy have increased number of mortars which have much annoyed our two posts of Cap Brun and Fort Mulgrave".[3] On December 12 a new Council of War was held, where it was decided to continue the old plan. Dugommier, however, seemed to doubt its success; his views were too pessimistic for a good general. On December 13 he wrote to the Comité " La moitié de cette armée est nulle, sans être connaisseur il ne faut que voir pour en être convaincu " . . . . . Les officiers ne valent pas leur subordinés. Les trois quarts ne s'occupent que de leurs plaisirs et de la nouvelle existence dont ils jouissent".[4] Duteil seemed to be in the same state of uncertainty and on December 14 he wrote to the Minister of War telling of the *canoniers* which were wanting etc.[4] Napoleon was confident. And holding an important position in the principal arm of a

---

[1] Archives de la Guerre.
[2] Hood in Gazette under date of December 13.
[3] Dundas in Gazette under date of December 12.
[4] Correspondance de Napoléon.

great siege, with 64 officers and 1600 men under him, and
but one old artillery general, with whom he was in the best
understanding over him, seeing his many and well placed
batteries taking a constantly increasing effect on the enemy
he could not but feel certain of success. On December 24
after the siege was over he wrote to Dupin "Je t'ai ·annoncé
de brillants succès et tu vois que je te tiens parole".[1] On
December 14 the final cannonading commenced, "A heavy
cannonade from and against Fort Mulgrave" as Hood wrote
in his Journal. The principal point of attack was Fort Mulgrave, and it was bombarded for three days. Thaon wrote
" Le feu était continuel et si violent que l'on comptait jusqu'à 7 bombes en l'air à la fois—La cannonade était vio-
lente. Tout était en jeu. La perte journalière était forte et
les troupes harassées de fatigue. Un feu continuel de 5 batteries de canon et de mortiers durait depuis 3 jours et 3
nuits contre les ouvrages de Balaguier. On s'attendait à une
attaque, on envoya un renfort de 350 hommes a Balaguier."
Further on he said " les defenses avaient été fort endomma-
gées par le feu ennemi". Victor wrote in his memoirs " l'ennemi ne restait point inactif. Après le feu terrible et
continuel que l'on faisait depuis plusieurs jours sur ses postes principaux, il s'attendait á une attaque générale". Dundas wrote "works (of Mulgrave) suffered much. The
number of men killed & disabled was considerable."[2] Langara wrote that Fort Mulgrave "which they had bombarded
and cannonaded from different quarters with the utmost
vivacity during the three preceding days[3] – – –" Smith
wrote[4] "As a prelude to the general assault the enemy directed an uninterrupted fire of shot and shells against the
Post of the Hauteur de Grasse for several days & nights.
The troops being unsheltered from the shells suffered much
and were so harrassed that it is not to be wondered at that

---

[1] Correspondance de Napoléon.
[2] Dundas to Henry Dundas, Dec. 20. Correspondence of Smith-Barrow.
[3] Langara to Alcudia. Dec. 21. St. Helens. R. O.
[4] Smith to Hamilton. Dec. 24. Correspondence of Smith-Barrow.

they were not able to resist the attack." I have quoted so much on the events and state of the army from the arrival of Dugommier up to the final attack on Fort Mulgrave, to show that in the siege of Toulon the artillery played by far the greatest part; that it was the one arm which inspired Dugommier with more or less confidence; that furthermore, it received from the corps of engineers under Marescot practically no support, and very little from the infantry, which was bad from the officers down; and that in the successful attack on Fort Mulgrave the greatest part of the credit falls to the artillery which for three days preceding had gradually destroyed the work and harrassed the garrison to such an extent that they were driven out by inferior infantry, and in spite of the fact that an attack was expected.

The final attack on Fort Mulgrave took place on December 17 [1] It had a garrison of about 700 men, made up of English, Spanish and Neapolitans. On the evening of 16th, about 7,000 of the best Republican troops were gathered at La Seyne. The plan was to make the attack in two columns, of about 2,000 men each, with a third column of about the same number as a reserve. Victor commanded the column which was to move along the coast of the promontory and attacking the fort on its right side, cut off all help which might be sent from Balaguier or Eguillette. The second column commanded by Brulé was to march against the front of the redoute. The reserve column was to hold itself ready to come to the assistance of whichever column needed it. It was a very stormy night, and at the last moment there was some hesitation as to whether the attack should

[1] For the final attacks, and departure of the Allies ;

Memoirs de Victor, Thaon, Napoléon. Relation de Marescot. Hood's Journal. Letters : Salicetti à Albitte, Archives Nationales AF II 2151 Langara to Alcudia, Dec. 21. St. Helens R. O. Dûgommier au M. de la Guerre Dec. 18. A. G. Barras Dec. 16. A. G. and Dec. 18. Recueil Aulard. Dundas in Gazette. Cook to Auckland Dec. 20. and Elliot to same, Dec. 24 Correspondence Auckland. Hood to Henry Dundas Dec. 20 ; Smith to Hood Dec. 20 ; David Dundas to Henry Dundas Dec. 20 ; and Smith to Hamilton Dec. 24. Correspondence of Smith ? Barrow.

be delayed until the next day or not. The Representants
and Dugommier each seemed anxious to shift the responsibility. Bonaparte's advice was to go ahead, as bad weather
was not at all disadvantageous for such an attack. The ex-
citement caused by uncertainty and impatience at last seized
them, and between one and two in the morning the signal
was given. The plan of attack was quite forgotten. The
fort was to be taken, and both columns, forming into one,
rushed forward in the true Republican revolutionary
manner straight for the fort. To the noise of the storm, the
cannon, and the Marseillaise, was added at the first resistance the usual cries of *sauve qui peut! à la trahison!* In this
way the cowardly tried to excuse their dastardly retreat.
The others, who were fortunately the greater part, pushed
on up to the reboute, where they were met with a determined resistance. Victor was wounded, and already Dugommier cried "je suis perdu!" and started for the reserve
column. It was already on its way, led on by Bonaparte
and an artillery captain Muiron, who knowing the ground
well, lead the advance guard. By a third and last effort
they entered the fort, and after a few minutes deadly fight
in the dark, the enemy retreated to Balaguier and Eguillette. At 4 o'clock the news reached Hood that Fort Mulgrave was taken. Bonaparte put Marmont, the future *duc de
Raguse* in charge of the artillery of the captured post and
directed him to turn the guns against the ships. In the
morning when the other troops at Balaguier and Eguillette
discovered the enemy in possession of Mulgrave they crowded
"to the water like the herd of swine, that ran furiously
into the sea possessed of the devil." [1] The ships and mortar
boats of the Allies bombarded Fort Mulgrave, but before
long the *Courageux* made the signal "wanting boat to tow".
Smith wrote, "The idea of *sauve qui peut* now seemed to possess everybody. the fleets of the different nations alarmed
at the idea of being burnt by red hot shot or shells from

---

[1] Account of Sir Sidney Smith.

Fort Mulgrave, Balaguier and Eguillette (now in possession
of the enemy) weighed anchor and crowded out of the road
in such haste as to alarm the troops on shore lest they
should be left behind."

This same morning Faron was attacked on three sides at
once, east, west and north. After some resistance and the
usual "*sauve qui peut!*" and "*à la trahison*", after which the
cowardly no longer impeded the advance, the Republicans
succeeded in establishing themselves there. "Lapoype tant
calomnieé s'est aussi parfaitement bien comporté". Thaon described this success as "aussi funeste qu'incroyable". Napoleon, after making his dispositions at Fort Mulgrave,
proceeded to turn his batteries on Fort Malbosquet, for although he felt certain that the Allies would soon evacuate
the city, he was determined that his shot and shells should
hasten their departure. Fréron wrote Dec 18 "Ils ont pris
des mesures pour mettre leur flotte à l'abri de nos canons
et de nos bombes qui n'ont cessé de les accablés". This
constant Artillery fire had a most demoralizing effect upon
the Allies. In the night of the 17th. they abandoned Fort
Malbousquet and Fort Pomets and very soon all the outside
posts were in the hands of the Republicans except Fort Mulgrave which the Allies were forced to hold to protect the em-
barcation.

As soon as the news reached Hood that Mulgrave was
taken a hurried council of war was called, on the morning
of the 17th. Hood, Langara, Gravina, Dundas, Elliot,
Thaon de Revel and others were present. The question was
whether after the loss of Balaguier and Faron it was advisable to hold the town. Hood and Gravina, counting upon
the reinforcements promised from Gibraltar, and on the 5000
Austrian troops who were on their way, voted for resistance,
but gave in at last to the opinion of the majority; which
was to abandon the city. It was decided; that the garrisons
of Malbousquet and Misiessy should hold out to the last extremity to cover the retreat; to inform the inhabitants that

the powers would use all means to carry away those who desire to leave the city; to embark the sick and wounded at once; to carry off the French vessels which remained armed during the siege and to destroy the others, as well as the *magasins de la Marine* and the arsenal. Immediately afterwards preparations were made for the embarkation although it was not until the next morning, Dec. 18 that the time was set. At first the inhabitants of the town, kept in ignorance of the intended departure, were quiet and orderly. The next day things began to change. As the Republicans drew nearer and nearer, as the troops were seen getting ready for departure in such large numbers, and especially as the shot and shell began to create havoc in the town and harbor, it dawned upon the inhabitants what was taking place. Then the wildest confusion reigned, some rushing to the shore for boats, others donning the red cockade, and vowing vengeance upon their fellow-citizens, who still remained royalists. Blood was shed in the streets between the rival factions. This state of affairs was rendered more terrible by the fire of the enemy. It will be remembered that Napoleon turned his batteries against Malbousquet after the fall of Mulgrave. He had said, a month before, that under such conditions Malbousquet would not hold out 48 hours. That evening it was evacuated, in spite of the formal orders of the council of war, that it was to be held. The further work of the artillery is well described by Thaon de Revel. "L'ennemi travailla à des batteries pendant tout la journée et la nuit (of the 17th) et les fit jour de bonne heure. (on the 18th) Les Français maîtres de l'artillerie qui était à Malbousquet canonnaient et bombardaient la ville. Ils avaient de même des encloué et tourné contre les Alliés toutes les bouches à feu des postes abandonnés. C' était un feu infernal et continuel contre la ville, la rade et le port". It was decided on the morning of the 18th to embark at 12 o'clock that night; but the constant advance of the Republicans upset the plans of the Allies somewhat and caused them to hasten their departure.[1] It took place in comparatively good order; the troops were all taken off without the loss of a man. This was not the case with the refugées; they hurried in large and terrified crowds to the water's edge: the war ships and all boats in the harbor were put at their disposal, but still many were lost in their wild flight by overcrowding the boats, and some of the boats were sunk by the shells of the enemy. The fact that 90 anchors were picked up in the harbor afterwards shows how quickly the boats must have departed. The whole affair was a terrible sight. Elliot wrote to Lady Elliot Dec 20. "There has seldom been crammed more misery and more terror in a short space than we have witnessed these last four days" . . . Fortunately the weather was good. "Had the weather been such as it has been ever since that is to say blowing strong from the eastward we must have all,— fleet, army and refugees inevitably perished". On the English and Spanish fleet were about 6000 refugees, who had been taken from the town. Some French accounts of Toulon contain long literary descriptions of the horrors of this day, and do not hesitate to follow them with a sharp condemnation of the action of the Allies, especially the English, in not taking off all the inhabitants. In the first place all detailed accounts of these incidents are more or less untrustworthy; to discriminate between the behavior of the Allies is quite wrong as no proof exists that the English were any less anxious to help the refugees than the Spaniards: they each had about an equal number on their fleets. De Brècy, *directeur des douanes royales* at Toulon, who was one of the fugitives wrote " L'Amiraux Hood, Goodal et Parker, Elliot et d'autres firent des offres les plus généreuses aux fugitifs. Le gouvernment anglais payait en outre tous les secours accordés aux fugitifs à Livourne, l'île d'Elbe et la Corse ".

Hood in Gazette under date Dec 20. " It became unavoidably necessary that the retreat should not be deferred beyond that night as the enemy commanded the town and ships by their shot and shell ".

As to taking them all off on such short notice it was next to impossible. Again these writers might, with more justice and far greater success, criticise and condemn the cruelty of the Republican army which made such a measure necessary in a civilized country at the end of the 18th century. It is true that Fox criticised the action of the English bitterly, but it was part of the plan of the opposition. "We do not know to what number but it is certain that thousands of poor wretches who have been deluded by our promises are now left by us to the guillotine. It must be a strong case of necessity which can justify such a proceeding . . ."

One thing remained still to be done before leaving the city, namely, to burn or destroy the ships, which could not be taken away, and the Arsenal. Sir Sidney Smith and the Adjutant of the Spanish navy were ordered to perform this duty. According to the agreement in the council of war it was to be done at the last moment, but they started either a little too late or the Republicans advanced a little too quickly. At all events Smith did not complete his work and the Spaniard did his stupidly. As Smith approached the Arsenal, preparing to burn everything, he found a number of the inhabitants, principally prisoners who had liberated themselves, ready to dispute him. The shouts of the Republicans could be heard not far off and the musket balls of the people in the town took effect. This delayed him somewhat, as did also a rather stupid act on the part of the Spaniards. They had been ordered to sink the ships in the basin, but finding it impracticable, they blew up two of the Frigates and in so doing sank two English gun boats, which were near, killing a lieutenant and several seamen. Smith wrote to Hood "Having now set fire to everything within our reach, exhausted our combustible preparations and our strength to such a degree that the men absolutely dropped on the oars, we directed our course to join the fleet running the gauntlet under a few ill directed shot from the forts Balgué and Aiguette". Langara wrote "In like manner

were blown up two Frigates loaded with 4000 Quintals of
Powder, on each of which a chemin de souffre was placed
by the Adjutant to the Squadron Don Francisco Riquelme
who acquired in that service the most distinguished honor,
as did likewise the other two officers who were exposed during a considerable time to the fire of Musquetry from the
Insurgents belonging to the Town".

On the morning of the 19th the Republicans entered Toulon. What the remaining inhabitants of the town had to
expect, is well shown by what the Representants wrote the
day preceeding. Barras wrote " L'infâme Toulon est à nous
rien ne peut le soutraire aux vengeances nationales. Demain le royaume de Louis XVII n'aura pas un pouce de
terre". [1] Picord, Frèron and Robespierre jeune wrote "demain nous serons dans Toulon occupés à venger la Republique" [2] The Republicans found a great deal of booty and
many provisions in Toulon. These were increased each day by
the ships which sailed in, thinking the city still in the hands
of the Allies. The booty was gathered together, sold and
the money divided among the soldiers. In the meantime
the executions took place. In general it was a repetition of
the punishment of Lyons; since thousands of the citizens
left with the Allies, those who remained behind had to take
their place, in spite of their remonstrances and declarations
of republicanism. The Representants wrote on Dec 20th[3]
" La vengeance nationale se deploie. L'on fusille à force.
Déja tous les officiers de la marine sont exterminés. La Republique sera vengée d'une manière digne d'elle. les mânes
des patriotes seront apaisées". As to the vessels which came
in daily; " Tout ce qui est etranger sur ses batiments est
fait prisonnier tout ce que est français est fusillé ". The representants were in their element. Nowhere did they display
their activity more than in " avenging the Republic ". After

---

[1] Barras 18th Dec. R. A.

[2] Letter 18th Dec. R. A.

[3] Recueil Aulard.

about a week they seemed to have had enough. On January 5th they wrote [1] " Hercule, dit-on, eut plus de peine à nettoyer les etables d'Angias qu'à dompter les lions et les monstres. Pour] nous nous preferons mille fois de nouvelles redoutes à attaquer plutôt que d'être condamnés à purger ce sol impur et grangrené. Nous se sommes entourés que de ruines, de supplices, de vengeances, de pleurs et de larmes que la rage du désespoire et non le repentir fait repandre".

The enemies of Bonaparte, and of his name, have tried to connect him with these orgies of the Representants. In 1814 the Baron d'Imbert published in a pamphlet on the siege of Toulon, which was nothing more than a praise of himself and other refugies, together with a bid for the favor of Louis XVIII, the following letter as written by Bonaparte. " Lettre de Bonaparte à la Convention. Citoyens Representants, C'est du champ de bataille, marchant dans le sang des traîtres que je vous annonce avec joie que vos ordres sont exécutés, et que la France est vengée. Ni l'âge, ni le sexe n'ont été épargnés: ceux qui avaient seulement été blessés par le canon republican ont été dépêchés par le Glaive de la liberté et par la bayonette de l'égalité. Salut et admiration. Signé, Bonaparte, citoyen sans-culottes. Others have said that of course Bonaparte must have taken part in the massacres as the artillery was used to execute the people "en masse". They seemed to forget that there were 160 other artillery officers under him. The above letter is, it seems to me, most decidedly a false one. Why should Bonaparte write to the Convention? Why should he sign himself simply "Bonaparte" as if he were known to all of them? Again had he, adopting the plan of the Representants, decided to distinguish himself in this manner, he would surely have received some mention from the Representants, at least from his friend Salicetti. Further, there is absolutely no

[1] Recueil Aulard.

other indication that he was a party to these executions.[1]
Like most of the officers, he propably looked upon them in
a cold half indifferent way, with some pity for the victims
and much contempt for the patriotic murderers. It must not
be expected that Bonaparte, brought up in the atmosphere
of the revolution, absorbed in his own ambition, and looking
on revolution as the means of satisfying it, should regard
such scenes with the same amount of human compassion
as one would expect to find in a man today. A letter which
he wrote at this time,[2] seems to indicate that he looked upon
such measures as so much a matter of course, as not to mention them, one way or the other; but that the first few days
he spent in examining the fortifications, and the naval and
military stores of Toulon. " Les Anglais n'ont fait que per-
fectionné et augmenté les fortifications de la place, ainsi Toulon est plus dans le cas de se defendre aujourd'hui que
jamais. . . . . Je m'occupe à faire construire les foures
à réverbère. . . . nous avons trouvé dans Toulon la
même artillerie qui y etait avant leur entrée. il nous reste
encore 15 vaisseaux." These few lines indicate that he was
occupied with quite different things than " avenging the republic ". The 15 vessels of which he spoke formed part of
those which took him later from this very port over to
Egypt.

---

[1] The Duc de Raguse says in his memoires that Napoleon opposed this
general execution of the people.
[2] Correspondance de Napoleon.

PART II.

DIPLOMATIC CORRESPONDENCE OF THE ALLIES AND RESULTS OF THE FALL OF TOULON.

CHAPTER I.

DISPUTE BETWEEN HOOD AND LANGARA—COMMISSIONERS AT TOULON—INSTRUCTIONS TO COMMISSIONERS—DECLARATION PUBLISHED AT TOULON—CORRESPONDENCE WITH AUSTRIA AS TO DECLARATION—CORRESPONDENCE WITH SPAIN AS TO DECLARATION—ENGLAND'S OBJECT IN HOLDING TOULON—PUBLICATION OF DECLARATION.

Toulon came into possession of the English so unexpectedly that Hood and others were quite unprepared with instructions relative to such an event. As Spain was much nearer, Langara received instructions early and the Spanish Court took such prompt measures as to procure them certain advantages which the English were afterwards unwilling to admit. Consequently there arose between these two powers disputes which lasted during the entire siege, and which were beginning to take dangerous proportions just as the fleets were forced to leave the harbor. Dundas wrote to O'Hara, Dec. 20 "[1] It must be remembered that from the manner in which Toulon came into His Majesty's possession it was impossible to be prepared with a force adequate to his wishes or to the importance of the acquisition;" and on the same day to Dundas [1] "you must be aware that Toulon came into our hands at a moment when it was impossible for us to have made any preparations for such an event." That the English were not quite satisfied with Hood's declaration has

[1] Letters from Sec. Dundas to Lieut. Gen. Dundas 1793–4 British Museum Mss. Addit. 27,594.

been seen. At first the English Admiral, Goodall, was appointed governor of the town, and the Spanish admiral, Gravina, commander of the garrison. Hood wrote September 14 [1] "We derive great assistance from Gravina who is the best sailor general imaginable; quick, intelligent, but not pretending to much military skill; and agreeing most cordially with the English." The Spanish believed that the command of the troops was to remain in their hands. St. Helens wrote, September 25; [2] "They (the Spanish troops) are to be accompanied by the marechal de Camp Don Rafael de Valdes (brother to the minister of the marine) who is to take the chief command of the troops on shore in the room of admiral Gravina. I heartily wish that he may succeeed equally well in maintaining a good understanding between the troops of the two nations." The English however did not care to have their forces (including those of their allies) under the command of a Spanish General and resorted to underhanded methods to avoid it. General O'Hara was to be sent as governor to Toulon, and on September 21 he was appointed a lieutenant-general; which rank made him superior to the Spanish commander whom he must consequently supercede. [3] In the meantime the dispute broke out between Hood and Langara. Langara wrote to Hood October 19; [4]

"Notwithstanding that the king is very well satisfied with the good conduct of rear-admiral Gravina during the time that he has been commandant general of the combined Troops at Toulon His Majesty, not to deprive the fleet of a general of his merit has resolved to relieve him from that command and that he should return to his ship to be employed in other important services, and has named Major-General Don Raphael Valdes to succeed him in the Command. I communicate it to your Excellency for your due

1 St. Helens to Grenville Sept. 25. R. O.

2 Record Office.

3 Dundas to O'Hara Nov. 30 Dundas to Gen. Dundas Dec. 20. British Museum Mss.

4 St. Helens to Grenville No. 8 R. O.

information and I hope that you will be pleased to give the
necessary orders as I have done for his being acknowledged".
Hood answered; "I return to your Excellency a thousand
thanks for your obliging communication of the arrival of
Don Valdes to take upon him the command of his Catholic
Majesty's troopes in the room of our most esteemed friend
admiral Gravina and have not a doubt but the service of
the common cause in which Spain and England are so very
cordially united will as cordially be carried on. I beg to offer
to your Excellency my sincere congratulations that Admiral
Gravina is going on so exceeding well".

It will be seen that the difference lay between Langara's
"commandant general of the combined troops" and Hood's
"the command of his Catholic Majesty's troops"; yet neither
admiral approached the question directly. A few days latter
however, Oct. 23, Langara informed Hood that Gravina had
been promoted to the rank of lieutenant-genneral of the fleet
and that the king had confirmed him [1] "the general command of the allied forces, in the possesssion of which he has
been by the agreement between your Excellency and me".
Major-general Valdes was to command the Spanish troops.
Hood no longer answered in an evading manner, but expressed himself so clearly as by no means to contribute to a
good understanding between the admirals: "No one can
more sincerely rejoice than myself at my much esteemed
friends promotion, but his Sardinian and Sicilian Majesty
having been graciously pleased to confide their respective
troops entirely to my disposal or to act under such british
officer as I may judge fit to put them I am very much at a
loss to conceive upon what ground Admiral Gravina can
take upon him the title of commander in chief of the combined forces at Toulon; more especially as the town and its
dependant forts were yielded up to the British alone and
taken possession of by me. I shall therefore feel it my duty
to put the Sardinian and Sicilian troops together with the

---

[1] Record Office. Letter published by Cottin.

british under the command of major general O'Hara, the
moment he arrives (who is now off the port) eventually subject
to such orders as I may see fit to give".[1] Then followed a
long letter from each of the admirals; Langara declared
that from the day they went on shore together, on Sept. 2,
it was agreed that the command should be divided. Hood
claimed that Toulon surrendered to him alone. This was
true, as the English officers had been on shore and had arranged for the surrender before the arrival of the Spaniards;
and the English fleet entered as soon as the Spanish was
seen in the distance; Hood did not dare enter before. It was
also true however that the Spaniards considered themselves
on an equal footing with the English and had exerted
themselves from the beginning upon this understanding.
St. Helens wrote to Grenville[2] " In general tho' this Court
certainly conceive themselves to be in strictness entitled to
the Nomination of the commander in chief of the forces on
shore, in virtue of the agreement to that effect, which they
suppose to have been concluded at the outset of the business
between the two admirals, it seems to me that they are by
no means disposed to insist pertinaciously upon that Claim,
being aware that it it can hardly be considered as reasonable now that the Spanish troops in the garrison bear so
small a proportion to those of Great Britain and her allies,
but their feelings are of course very deeply wounded by those
expressions in Lord Hood's letter to Admiral Langara on
the 25th of October which so positively assert that the rights
which have been acquired over the town and port of Toulon with its ships belong not to the two crowns jointly but
solely and exclusively to Great Britain, contrarary to the notions which have been hitherto entertained by this government, which they have so ostentatiously announced to their
subjects and in consequence of which they have made such
great and expensive efforts for the securing that important

---

[1] Record Office. Published by Cottin.
[2] St. Helens to Grenville, Nov. 8. R. O.

possession and I therefore cannot help taking the liberty of expressing a wish that their share in this joint right may at least nominally be preserved to them, since otherwise there is reason to fear that besides their withdrawing immediately from Toulon all their ships and land forces the effect of our late endeavors to cultivate a good understanding with them will be entirely lost and that they will cease to look towards England with any kind of cordiality or confidence." This was his official report; the same day he wrote to Grenville[1] "I am more anxious than I can express that for the reasons mentioned in my dispatch some means may be found for calming the very great degree of pique and ill-humor which this court have conceived on account of the Toulon business, by giving them at least nominally an equal share with us in the Possession or Trusteeship of that place and its appertenances. It is certainly true that at the outset of the enterprise Admiral Langara had great reason to presume that it was upon that footing that he had been invited to concur in it: witness his joint proclamation with Lord Hood, the ceremonies of the landing etc. Besides which even supposing that the motives which he and his court entertained upon that head were founded merely upon self delusion, we certainly were not ignorant that they acted from the impulse of that conception however erroneous, and therefore the deferring to undeceive them till the precise moment when their services were no longer needed would surely have an appearance, if not of ill-faith at least of Machiavelism, which would ill accord with the general character of the British Government. The Duke de la Alcudia seems to wish for some written agreement upon this subject but I imagine that that will hardly be found practical." These two letters just given show that even the English ambassador at Madrid saw the justice of the Spanish claims. This dispute continued during the entire time of the occupation of Toulon, but before following it further it is necessary to speak of the Commision which was sent by the English to Toulon.

1 Helens to Grenville Nov. 8. R. O.

O'Hara had been appointed Governor of Toulon before the end of September; and Sir Gilbert Elliot, who was to have been governor of Dunkirk, was sent out also to take charge of the civil affairs. O'Hara and Elliot were to form with Hood a joint commission for the government of Toulon. Elliot left England the 11th of October, but it was not until the 22nd that Grenville, after consulting Pitt, informed the Court of Madrid, through St. Helens, of the appointment of this commission.[1] To settle on the spot such questions as may arise, His Majesty has " in execution of the trust undertaken in His name by Lord Hood authorized Sir Gilbert Elliot to proceed to Toulon to act conjointly with His Majesty's officers commanding his sea and land forces in the execution of a Commission respecting all the points of a Civil nature which may present themselves in the course of events at Toulon. His Majesty has also in consequence of the surrender of that place and from the sense of the necessity of relieving Admiral Goodall from the duties of a situation incompatible with the naval service, appointed Lieutenant-General O'Hara to succeed that officer as Governor of Toulon, and to take upon him the command of His Majesty's forces in that part of France. Lord Hood, Sir Gilbert Elliott and General O'Hara are severally directed to maintain the most cordial and confidential intercourse with the Persons employed by his Catholic Majesty, and to endeavor to the utmost to continue that good understanding which has hitherto prevailed there so much to the advantage of the common cause."

The foregoing was inserted in a letter to St. Helens on Pitt's advice. Pitt wrote October 17 to Grenville;[2] " We think there ought to be a sentence inserted distinctly mentioning that we have appointed a governor of Toulon in consequence of the place being surrendered to us; adding, of course, every proper assurance of our desire to cooperate with Spain in that question. We must take this line respect-

---

1 Grenville to St. Helens Oct. 22. R. O.

2 Pitt to Grenville Oct. 17. Mss. of Fortesque.

ing Toulon whenever any question occurs between us and Spain on that subject." Pitt foreseeing the possible objection of Spain added, "The sooner this step is taken, the more likely to avoid disgust". Henry Dundas wrote to Grenville[1] "It occurs to Mr. Pitt and to me that it is better not to keep back our having appointed a governor. The grounds on which we obtained possession, and the impossibility of Hood and the officers acting under him continuing to exercise the office and duties of Governor, are reasons too obvious for adopting the measure to be concealed".

Buckingham wrote to Grenville, asking about the division of command and added refering to the French ships at Toulon, [2]" it does not seem wise to risk the only safe deposit which the war has placed our hands". The foregoing, as well as the tardiness in informing Madrid of the measures taken in London, shows that the English government was not dealing openly with Spain in reference to Toulon.

On Oct. 18 long and detailed instructions were sent to the English Commissioners at Toulon. The substance of these was as follows. [3] The possession of Toulon and the prospect of its extensive consequences in the South of France have given occasion for the Commission. It is to have three principal objects; 1st, to govern Toulon; 2nd, (" which is more extensive and more important ") to induce other parts of France to have recourse to His Majesty's protection; to aid in the re-establishment of a regular government which is to end the internal disorders in France and open the way to a satisfactory termination of the war: 3rd., to take charge of any provinces or districts which should be occupied by his Majesty's arms or place themselves under his protection, "till some regular and general system shall have been re-established and a regular and a definite pacification concluded". The Commission is also to publish immediately,

---

1 Dundas to Grenville Oct. 20. Mss. of Fortesque.
2 Buckingham to Grenville Oct. 24th. Mss. Fortesque.
3 Record Office. Published almost in full by Cottin.

and in His Majesty's name, a declaration addressed to the people of Toulon, "according to the tenor of the paper herewith transmitted". The powers of the other members of the commission must not interfere with the authority of the military governor in any matters of military detail. As far as is consistent with this principle, due regulations ought to be framed for protecting as far as possible the persons of the inhabitants and for providing for the ordinary course of justice in civil affairs. The possibility of retaining the inhabitants in their civil and military employments must depend upon the dispositions they manifest and upon circumstances. The suffering of public meetings, or of authorizing and recognizing the deliberations of any committee must be governed by similar circumstances. A power must be exercised wherever it is necessary of confining, or sending away, suspected persons. "On all these points it is impossible to form specific instructions; the Commissioners will jointly exercise their discretion." The second general head of instructions gives the following : His Majesty's primary object is to terminate the war as speedily as possible. Whatever may be the form of government in France His Majesty will feel himself entitled to demand such terms as may afford to himself and his allies reasonable indemnification for the past and security for the future. His Majesty is not disposed to prescribe any particular form, he is persuaded it is only on the foundation of hereditary monarchy (subject to such limitations as may be found advisable) that a rational prospect at present exists of any regular government being reestablished. All parts of France which may wish to deliver themselves from the tyrany of the present rule and concur in the restoration of a regular government, on the foundation of hereditary monarchy and accept His Majesty's protection, shall be well governed, and restored at the conclusion of a definite treaty of peace, "unless by the terms of such treaty it shall be agreed that any such place or district shall, for the purpose of indemnification or secur-

ity be ceded to any of the powers who are engaged in concert with His Majesty in the present war. No idea is entertained of pushing that principle to the extent of proposing any plan of partition or dismemberment applicable to the interior of France ; but it can only relate to such possessions on the frontiers as shall appear on fair discussion to come within the real objects which are professed. As this consideration is naturally more applicable to Austria than to any other continental power it does not appear that in the south of France, this exception can be material with respect to any district but such as may be contiguous to the frontier either of Spain or Sardinia, or possibly Switzerland, in case the Cantons may be brought to take an active part in the war". No alarm is to be created from the idea of extensive projects of aggrandizement and dismemberment such as are not in His Majesty's contemplation. The declaration which you are to publish at Toulon will be circulated as speedily as possible in the interior of France. You will be particularly careful to state on all occasions His Majesty's conviction that the acknowledgement of a hereditary monarchy, affords the only probable ground for restoring regular government in France. His Majesty is far from meaning to pledge himself to any approbation of the articles of the Constitution of 1789 and is on the contrary persuaded that every part of the French nation which wishes for the reestablishment of Monarchy will ultimately see the impossibility of retaining many parts of that constitution, yet His Majesty has not felt this as any reason for withholding his protection from the people of Toulon, under the circumstances in which it was sought for. Under the third head of instructions is found: ' all such places as choose to put themselves under the protection of His Majesty will be governed under His " general superintending power", but this authority must be subject to no fixed limitations, and must in time of war be inforced wherever it is necessary, by the military power. [1] " The Re-establishment of the former

---

[1] Following not published by Cottin.

modes of Judicature, of the former Ecclesiastical establishment and particularly of the Provincial states in the provinces where they existed in a known and established form previous to the late troubles seem likely if they should be found practicable to be productive of great advantage and to lead to the restoration of Order and good government. [1] But even in looking to these objects great caution will be necessary not to do violence to existing prejudices and it may be necessary unless the minds of the people at large should be disposed to such measures as I have stated, to postpone them for a time and to make no alteration in whatever may be the Train and order of things which you may find existing father than is necessary for the fundamental object of acknowledging a monarchical government." [2] " The measures to be taken with respect to property which has been confiscated, and afterwards sold under the authority of the Convention, as well as that which may belong to persons who may continue in hostility to His Majesty ; with respect to the circulation or suppresion of assignats, and also with respect to the collection and appropriation of any public revenues, are also points of so much delicacy, and may depend so much on local circumstances, that it is not thought right, at present to make them the subject of positive instructions." – – – –

This resumé of the instructions sent to the Commissioners at Toulon shows the ideas of Pitt, and the political views of the English at this time.

The declaration which was published at Toulon differed from that of Hood in two particulars: 1st; His Majesty was not willing to commit himself to the constitution of 1789, but simply regarded the reestablishment of an hereditary monarchy as the necessary form of stable government with

---

[1] This proposal to reestablish the old provincial states as well as the idea that the people of the South of France would care very little what was taken on the frontiers or in the North shows that the new spirit which was awakened in the large majority of the French people was ill understood in London.

[2] Following published by Cottin.

which he hoped to make peace. He did not wish to specify any particular form nor to interefere with the internal affairs of France. 2nd; It was expressly stated that at the termination of a treaty of peace His Majesty expected for himself and his allies a just indemnification for the costs and dangers of a war which was forced upon him by France. This declaration had been drawn up after a diplomatic correspondence with the courts of Austria, Spain and Sardinia. On Sept. 14 information was sent to Sir Morton Eden in Vienna that a public declaration would be made as to His Majesty's views on the war with France. On Sept. 25 Eden wrote to Grenville, 'that Thugut had informed him that Austria agreed not to take any step toward the interior arrangement of France [1] "without a previous and confidential communication with his Majesty — — — — — — — Sentiments entertained here were he (Thugut) added that France should be so far weakened as no longer to be dangerous. — — — — — — — On the subject of Indemnification the acquisition for Great Britain being to be looked for in the Foreign settlements and Colonies of France, no jealousy, he observed, nor clash of interests could arise." On Sept. 27 Grenville forwarded a draft of the proposed declaration to Eden. Speaking of the form of govenment in France[1] "it is infinitely better that this should be left to the feelings and experiences of the French nation itself than that Foreign Powers should seek to impose ¦upon that country particular points with respect to the modification of a monarchical government to which it may still be adverse. — — — — — the claim for indemnification is no less carefully attended to. It appeared neither necessary nor advisable to specify particular objects of indemnification because these must of necessity depend on the events of the war. — — — — If on the whole the proposed declaration should meet with the concurrence of that Court it will be right for you to lose no time in returning the Messenger in order that it may be published in His Majesty's name."

---

1 Record Office.

On Oct. 12 Eden sent off his answer in which he said that the Austrian minister agreed with the declaration but speaking of the indemnification wished [1] " that the expression ' telles que les Puissances Belligerantes ne peuvent se dispenser de demander' might be omitted, as it might give a handle to all those who are engaged either actively or only apparently in the war, equally to bring forward claims of indemnification and increase the difficulties of the pacification. The King of Prussia would, he (Thugut) said, be the first to found on it pretensions for the further aggrandizement to which this court could never assent, till it has itself made acquitions equal to those of His Imperial Majesty in Poland. In the place of these words he proposed to insert ' Sa Majeste ne peut se dispenser etc'. I told him that I would transmit his observations for your Lordship's consideration tho' I could not agree with him in the propriety of the change proposed, as in a declaration of this kind the making no mention of the other Belligerent Powers might give them umbrage, might make them apprehensive of a separate peace without any attention to their interests & consequently render them less inclined to cooperate heartily towards the termination of the war. The invitation to France to follow the example of the inhabitants of Toulon, he said he looked upon to be salutary as much as it regarded the towns situated at a distance from those parts to which his Imperial Majesty's views of indemnification were directed; but he trusted that should Lille or any other place contiguous to the Belgic provinces offer to surrender to His Majesty on the same conditions as Toulon that His Majesty would look upon himself as an auxiliary Power on that side of France, and consider them as being to form the future Barrier of those provinces, would accept them for the Emperor & to be governed in His name till the Peace. This afternoon I waited again by appointment on M. de Thugut who delivered me a copy which I have the honor to inclose, of the Emperors proposed declaration. In reading over the

[1] Record office.

paper I pointed out to him the words "par les moyens que les lois fondamentales de sa constitution autorisent". I wished him to supress them as they appeared to go beyond your Lordship's meaning & they might be construed to imply an intention to interfere in the internal arrangement of France & I particularly insisted on the advantage of a perfect union of sentiment on this important point of the declaration. He however adhered to these words as being more consistent with the form of government of his Imperial Majesty's Dominions—I spoke again to M. de Thugut on the subject of Prussia and Sardinia. As to the former I had the satisfaction to find him disposed could the King of Prussia's effective cooperation for the conquest of Alsace and Loraine be absolutely secured to recommend to the Emperor to make a formal renunciation of any exchange whatsoever for Bavaria but in such a form as may save the Emperor's dignity. [1] He seemed however to have but little hopes of any effective support being procured from Prussia which opinion he considered as sufficiently justified by the events of the Campaign. Offers of futher assistance may he thinks be made, but he expects to find them clogged with such proposals of compensation as cannot be admitted in order that the refusal may be seized as a pretext to withdraw from the war. [2] He added that his expectation would be fully gratified if it could be possible to obtain from His Prussian Majesty His several contingents to the King, the Emperor and the Empire".

The foregoing gives one a further insight into the political relations at the time of the King's declaration. The English Court was anxious to act in consert with the Austrian in taking this step and had awaited her answer before publishing the declaration. It was not quite so particular about

---

[1] It is interesting to see how under the influence of England Thugut is willing to modify his policy.

[2] As early as 1793 Thugut seemed to have foreseen the possibility of a "Treaty of Basel."

Spain. This is shown by the fact that the draft of the declaration was sent a week later to Lord St. Helens, and that his answer would not necessarily be waited for before publishing the declaration. This is another proof that England was less open to the Spanish Court than to the Austrian, even on the subject of Toulon where the two Courts were supposed to act in consert. The communication to St. Helens is dated October 4. It ran as follows: [1] " I transmit to your Excellency by His Majestys command the draft of a declaration which his Majesty proposes to publish for the purpose of explaining to the well disposed part of the French nation His Majestys views with respect to the prosecution of the present war. The circumstances of the late transaction at Toulon and the great probability that a similar disposition exists in many parts of France, have induced His Majesty to believe that the present moment is favorable for a declaration of this nature. It is uncertain whether the rapid succession of events by which the present crisis is marked may not render it expedient not to delay the publication of this paper till an answer can be received from the Spanish government respecting its contents. But even in that case His Majesty has felt that an early and confidential communication of it to the Court of Madrid was an attention on his part due to the union and friendship subsisting between the two crowns, and in case circumstances should admit of the delay, His Majesty will be extremely desirous of receiving from the Catholic King the fullest communication of His sentiments respecting it. His Majesty flatters himself that in all events the principles manifested in that declaration are such as will be found to correspond entirely with those of His Catholic Majesty. I feel it unnecessary for me to enter into any detailed discussion of these, as the paper itself will naturally suggest to your Excellency what is to be said upon it.—You will not fail to remark that in any intervention respecting the in-

---

[1] Record Office.

terior of France the King looks rather at the affording support to well disposed persons in that Kingdom than to the establishing there by external force any particular government. In recommending to the French to unite in the cause of monarchy His Majesty advises that only, which seems essentially necessary to the re-establishment of external or internal tranquility, but carefully avoids discussing the various modifications and limitations of that form. His Majesty is persuaded that the entire re-establishment of an arbitrary Monarchy there, is neither practicable nor desirable. His Majesty is on the other hand far from approving as an ultimate state of things the constitution accepted by the late King during the constraint which followed His being brought back from Varennes. But all the particular details of any intermediate system must as it appears be left to the discussion of the French themselves and foreign powers have no immediate object in looking farther than to the general principles stated in the inclosed draught. With respect to the principle of indemnification I have before stated to your Excellency that His Majesty in asserting His right on that subject as resulting from the unprovoked aggression of France admits in the most express manner the right of Spain founded on the same rule of equity and reason. His Majesty even authorizes you to assure the court of Madrid of his sincere disposition to co-operate with that court as far as circumstances will permit in the attainment of such objects as His Catholic Majesty may have in view for that purpose. And His Majesty will receive with satisfaction and return with openness any confidence which the King of Spain may be disposed to place in His Majesty on that subject. Nothing could be more pleasing to His Majesty than to see the union and cordiality which has subsisted between the naval and military forces of the two Crowns on the occasion of the late event of Toulon. His Majesty flatters himself that the result of that transaction must lead to establishing a still more intimate union between the two courts as well as among those who are respectively employed by them.—it is obviously to be desired that the combined forces of the powers engaged in the war against France should be enabled to profit of further openings and to make Toulon a center of operations which may extend themselves as far as possible in the South of France where so much disposition exists to favour the cause of monarchy". On Oct. 30 St Helens answered [1] "Alcudia has acquainted me verbally that His Majesty's intended Declaration to the French Nation has been read by His Catholic Majesty with much satisfaction" The Spanish were preparing a similar declaration. On Nov. 8 St. Helens wrote further that the declaration of Spain was quite satisfactory and corresponded with the English. As to the indemnification; [1] "Your Lordship will observe that the Duke de la Alcudia's Letter admits and recognizes the justice of that Claim in the fullest and most explicite terms so that a discussion of the details of that subject may now be brought forward whenever circumstances may render such a measure advisable." The following is an extract from Alcudia's Letter. [1] "With respect to the point of indemnity it appears to the King to be just that England should demand it for the expenses of the war which the French themselves have declared and His Majesty would contribute so far as he may be able to its being realized, at the same time that His Majesty claims the rights which in like manner belong to him upon the self-same ground, being well assured that both sovereigns will co-operate with mutual good faith in forwarding the just views which each of them may propose to himself on the point in question."

Alcuda stated also that the Spanish King was quite satisfied with the declaration. On Nov. 30 Grenville wrote to St. Helens [1] "Monsieur del Campo having communicated to me the draughts of the proposed declaration to be published,

[1] Record Office.

by the court of Madrid I assured him in general terms of the King's approbation of that paper and your Excellency will not fail to express the same sentiments to the Duke of Alcudia. It has however not escaped the attention of this court that while in a letter written to you as well as in other communications between the two governments the principle of indemnity is not only recognized by the court of Madrid but it is even insisted upon as applicable to the situation of Spain no notice is taken of any views of this nature in the declaration which is to be addressed to the people of France. Whatever may be the real views of Spain in this respect it seems very desirable that the Spanish Government should if possible be brought to enter into some explanation of this kind on that important and delicate point. —With respect to the indemnity of Spain, your Excellency will take an early opportunity to enter into some explanation with the Duke of Alcudia on this subject and you will endeavor to convey to him in a general manner such as may not excite jealously His Majesty's wish that in the result of the war the Spanish indemnity may be acquired on the frontier of France, by which means Spain would obtain a great and valuable accession of strength, particularly as to means of defense and would no longer be exposed to the invasion of France and continue thereby in some degree dependent on that Country. Your Excellency's ability and experience will suggest to you the means of placing this proposal in its most favorable lights and of supporting it by the arguments the most likely to make impression. In asking this explanation and in urging this proposal it will be proper that your Excellency should avow, on His Majesty's part, that the indemnity to this country can be found only in the French Possessions out of Europe, and you will therefore employ all your attention to convince the Spanish minister how little cause of jealousy to the Court of Spain arises from such acquisition, the immense territorial possessions of Spain in America are such as to furnish ample

scope for the exertions of all the industry, capital and skill
which Spain can employ and any acquisitions particularly
in the Leeward Islands may truly be stated as being much
less desirable to Her than to any other of the European Nations. His Majesty conceives therefore and you will urge it
as a proposal to the Spanish Ministers that both courts may
with advantage further the views of each other in the points
above mentioned. His Majesty by exerting His influence at
the peace as far as circumstances will then admit, for procuring to Spain a valuable accession of territory on the frontier of France; and the Court of Spain by favoring in the
like manner His Majesty's views of acquisition in the Leeward Islands. With respect to St. Domingo it is conceived
that the views of Spain may not unreasonably be turned to
that Quarter, and altho' the small advantage which Spain
actually derives from the part of that Island now in His
possession might seem to afford a sufficient reason against
Her looking to further acquisition there, yet it is probable
that views of that sort are in fact entertained both by the
hope of advantage and also as a means of deriving security
against the dangers with which the Spanish colonies are
menaced from the establishment of the principles on which
the French have lately acted in the West Indies, and particularly in St. Domingo. You will be aware that His Majesty's views also are in part directed towards that island, but
it is by no means conceivable that these projects entertained
by the two Courts are incompatible with each other. The
extent of that Island and the distance of the Spanish Quarters from the parts nearest to Jamaica leaving full scope for
arrangements being taken in concert respecting this Island
such as may be mutually beneficial to both Countries. It is
not the King's pleasure that you should actually propose
any precise plan for this purpose or indeed any positive
agreement with respect to the other objects of indemnification above mentioned, but it is judged to be extreemely important for His Majesty's service that your Excellency should

without delay enter into explanations on these points with
the Spanish government, and endeavour to learn to what extent the Court of Madrid would be disposed to enter into engagements with His Majesty on the principles already laid
down, and that you should transmit to me an account of the
result of your conferences on this subject in order that a
judgment may be formed of the best manner of bringing
forward those discussions which the situation of Two Courts
in the present moment seems to render indispensable".

In another letter of the same date Grenville wrote: " With
respect to the political considerations with which this business is connected, I have in my other dispatch of this date
stated to you at large the sentiments and views of His Majesty as to the general State of affairs, but I think it right in
this place to give Your Excellency the fullest authority for
entering into unreserved Explanations with the Spanish
Government on the subject of Toulon. His Majesty has in
no case any view respecting that place different from that
which has already been avowed in His name: That at the
Conclusion of Peace that Port should be restored to the
Crown of France, and that in the Interval it should serve
in His Majesty's Hands as a means of carrying on the war,
and as a Pledge of indemnity to Him and His allies, including in that Description the Crown of Spain whose claim
to Indemnity His Majesty has already distinctly avowed."[1]
Before its publication the declaration had also been communicated to the Sardinian Court, " as additional proof of
confidence".

On November 20 the declaration was published at Toulon. Elliot wrote November 23. In regard to the ships [2] " the
words "ont été rendus" appeared to give a little uneasi-
ness to one or two members of the deputation as it conveyed
something mortifying to their national spirit. I therefore
substituted the word " confiés", which gave entire satisfac-

---

[1] These lines state clearly England's intentions at Toulon.
[2] Record Office. Commissioners to Toulon 1793. Hood, Elliot, O'Hara.

tion and is at the same time consonant with the truth ".

It is hoped that the foregoing extracts have given a clear idea of the circumstances under which this declaration arose. It may be regarded as the official statement of England's intentions in the beginning of the War of the First Coalition. As the fortunate termination of this war was regarded as near at hand, this declaration was to form a preliminary basis for the peace negotiations. Austria and Spain had agreed to it. It was not communicated to Prussia. It was Pitt who really framed the declaration, and his idea was to treat with any kind of a stable government in France. Her internal affairs as long as she remained quiet were a minor consideration. The "indemnification" was the main object in London as also in Vienna and Madrid. On October 5 Pitt wrote to Grenville [1] " We can treat with any form of regular government if it be solidly established". Austria, however, was somewhat concerned as to the internal government of France, and it was out of consideration for her that England declared for hereditary monarchy. This difference in the drafts of the declaration had been noticed by Elliot, who wrote to Secretary Dundas on October 18 : [2] " The declaration as at last settled by you and Pitt differs from the last draft as to the following words, " Quand la paix sera faite (et Sa Majesté declare par la presente qu'elle sera prête à la faire aussitôt qu'un gouvernement regulier sera établi en France)". The words in the draft as last settled are " Whenever the Hereditary Monarchy of France shall be restored & a Treaty of Peace concluded - - -".

The English Government has been reproached for not making this declaration agree entirely with the proclamation of Lord Hood, and with his understanding with the people of Toulon. In the first place, Hood acted without positive instructions, and more or less on his own responsibility ; again, Toulon was not at that moment in a condition to give

[1] Mss. Fortesque.
[2] Commissioners to Toulon.

the people a right to expect England, or any nation, to accept their terms unconditionally. Hood might possibly have avoided the phrase " the Constitution of 89 "; but the fact that he did not was not sufficient reason for the English to withdraw from the city, rather than commit themselves to a form of government which might have made a future peace impossible. England's object was to allow such latitude in this respect as to win over the greatest number of the inhabitants of France. " A stable form of government " was Pitt's idea, but it was finally agreed to insist upon " hereditary monarchy ".

Although England had now come to a definite understanding with her allies Austria and Spain, there were still a number of questions pending between the different Courts; questions which excited jealousy and distrust, and thereby prevented combined action. Had the Allies put as much thought into their military operations as is found in their diplomatic negotiations, this vast scheme of indemnification might have been realized; but at Toulon, as elsewhere, the reckless Republican army, directed by a few men of genius, above all by Napoleon, proved more than equal to the disunited Allies. Three disputed questions preoccupied the courts at London and Madrid. First, were the Spanish to be on an equality with the English in the Government of Toulon? Second, what was to become of the French ships in case the Allies were forced to retire? Third, were the brothers of the late King to be permitted to enter the city in an official capacity, or at all? Finally, the question of the Austrian reinforcements, which were promised but failed to arrive, became a serious one between the courts of London and Vienna. The first stages of the dispute between England and Spain as to the command at Toulon have already been mentioned, and will be further spoken of in connection with the questions of the French princes, and of the fleet.

CHAPTER II.

QUESTION OF THE FRENCH PRINCES—END OF DISPUTE AS TO
AUTHORITY AT TOULON—QUESTION OF THE EMIGRANTS
—THE AUSTRIAN REINFORCEMENTS.

Quite early the English government received intimation
that the French Princes wished to go to Toulon. On October
2 St. Helens wrote [1] "The Agents of the French Princes are
extremely desirous to obtain permission for Monsieur to repair immediately to Toulon, and I am afraid that the Spanish Minister has given but too much encouragement to this
idea although I have written to engage him to lay it aside,
at least for the present". On October 18 the Spanish Minister in London, Marquis del Campo, wrote to Grenville, and
speaking of the affair of Toulon as a [2] "nouveau chemin pour
parvenir au grand but de calmer les troubles qui agitent et
dechirent la France", and as "ce grand point d'appui pour
regenerer la monarchie francaise", claimed that England and
Spain "se trouvent dans l'obligation de proportionner tout
soutien et toute aide sinon à son captif monarque Louis XVII,
au moins à celui qui se trouve à même de representer sa
Personne".—"Les pretentions de l'Oncle du Roy doivent
par consequent être regardées comme justes".—"Il faut
qu'il soit reconnu à Toulon en qualité de Regent de France.
Ce Prince se trouvant sur le lieu—pourra agir d'une manière active, augmenter le parti du Roy, s'attirer les esprits
encore vacillants et contribuer personelle et efficacement à
voir realiser les intentions des Puissances.—Par ce moyen
nos deux souverains auront la gloire d'avoir posé les pre-
miers fondemens de la Paix dans le Royaume en établissant
dans la dite ville le plus proche Parent de son monarque
legitime : celui-ci benira éternellement les auteurs de son
bonheur et les deux puissances alliés auront encore la satis-

---

[1] Record Office.
[2] Record Office. St. Helens' papers.

faction d'avoir triomphé par sa puissance et sa justice de tous les efforts de l'iniquité.—C'est par les ordres express de ma Cour que j'ai l'honneur de transmettre à V. Exce. ces considerations—Le Roy mon maitre se flatte de trouver en elle (Sa M. Britannique) la même manière de penser et les mêmes dispositions à soutenir Monsieur dans Toulon, favorisant de toutes les manières possibles son établissement dans la dite ville, et ses progrès dans cette partie de la France".

It may be readily seen that del Campo's arguments would not appeal to the English government. On October 22 Grenville wrote to St. Helens "It is by no means part of His Majesty's plan to exclude the late King's brother from taking such share in the final arrangement of that business (the internal affairs of France) as even in the intermediate measures leading to it as their situation and events which may arise in the interior of France may hereafter point out. But when the circumstances which have attended the surrender of Toulon are taken into consideration it must surely be felt that the admitting the French Princes into that Port is a step leading to the most material and important consequences, and which cannot be taken without mature deliberation. His Majesty is by no means an advocate of the Constitution of 1789 and is on the contrary persuaded that no persons sincerely wishing the restoration of Monarchy in France can ultimately wish that it should rest on so precarious and insecure a footing. But it must not be forgotten that the people of Toulon have declared for Monarchy as established by that Constitution, and in consequence of that declaration put themselves under the King's protection; that under that Constitution as finally settled, the Comte de Provence has no absolute claim to the Regency nor can the office of Lieutenant-General be conferred on the Comte d'Artois. And that in general the situation of the French Princes and the conduct, principles and supposed resentments of the persons by whom they are surrounded cannot be considered as likely in the present moment to conciliate the minds of the inhabitants of that place. There is besides an essential and necessary condition before the King can consent to join His measures to those of the French Princes to the degree that would be done by admitting them into Toulon. It is indispensable that they should enter into previous explanation respecting the principle of pacification and that they should recognize the justice of the claim of His Majesty and His Allies, including the Catholic King to a fair indemnification for the risques, expenses and losses of a war commenced by the unjust aggression of France. His Majesty by no means wishes the Court of Madrid to understand this communication as meant to operate as a final bar to the idea of employing the French Princes in France and particularily in the South. But His Majesty expects that no step towards this important determination should be taken, but in consert, and He thinks it absolutely necessary to ascertain beforehand, first whether the appearance of the Princes at Toulon would in fact be advantageous or prejudicial to the common interests in the present moment. Secondly whether the Princes themselves are disposed to act reasonably and according to the exigencies of the moment relative to the interior of France; whether they and those who advise them are sensible of the necessity of laying aside animosities and resentments of waving inadmissable claims, and of submitting to be guided in their conduct by those powers whose support they ask, and lastly whether they are ready to enter into full and unequivocal explanation respecting the principles of indemnification above stated". It is interesting to compare this communication, inspired by Pitt, with the foregoing sentimental note from Del Campo.

The English had taken prompt and decided measures to prevent the Spaniards from sharing their authority at Toulon, and they were naturally determined not to allow Monsieur to procede to that place as regent. On October 22, the same day as the foregoing communication was sent to Lord St. Helens, instructions[1] were forwarded to Francis Drake, (the English representative at Genoa, where Monsieur was supposed to go previous to embarking for Toulon,) to inform Monsieur of the impossibility of his proceeding to Toulon; of "the inconvenience which would result, both personally to that prince, and also to the general interests from any eclat taking place on this subject"; and also of the question of its being "agreeable to the inhabitants of Toulon". Further if Monsieur insisted, Drake was to inform the Commissioners at Toulon that they were not authorized to permit him to enter without having first received instructions from His Majesty . . . . . "but you (Drake) will use every endeavour in your power by respectful and conciliatory representations, to prevent recourse being had to this extremity, and you will endeavour to persuade the ministers of the allied powers at Genoa to support you in these representations". Meanwhile Monsieur, being in secret communication with Spain, took the matter into his own hands, and informed the English government through the Duc d'Harcourt, the representative of the Princes in London, of his decision to proceed to Toulon to assume the duties of regent. The English court was determined to prohibit him. On November 30. instructions[2] were sent to the Commissioners at Toulon not to admit him. On the same day orders were hurried to John Trevor in Turin to stop Monsieur as he passed through the city: to say to His Sardinian Majesty that it is impossible for Monsieur to go there without the approbation of the King of Great Britain.[3] "If Monsieur should have already quitted Turin previous to your receiving this despatch you will urge the King of Sardinia to send after him some proper person for the purpose of making these representations both in the King's name and in that

---

[1] Record Office. Published by Cottin.
[2] Commissioners to Toulon. Record Office.
[3] Foreign Office, Sardinia. Record Office.

of the King of Sardinia and in order if possible to prevent
the eclat which must arise from Monsieurs persisting in His
project and being exposed to a public refusal on the part of
His Majesty's officers at Toulon". Long and precise instructions were sent to St. Helens, by Grenville. on November 30.[1]
"With respect to the great question of a recognition of the
authority of Monsieur as Regent, it seems to depend in a
great degree upon the result of discussions of the nature already mentioned and also upon the course of events to
which the war may give rise. His Majesty is by no means
adverse to this recognition but in order that it should be
rendered advantageous to the common cause it must be
combined both with circumstances in the interior of France
favorable to it, and also with such explanations on the part
of the Princes as may shew that their views are not in opposition to those of the principal Powers of Europe, whose
aid they seek, and that they are willing rather to listen to
the advice of those Powers and to yield to the necessity of
the existing circumstances than to give scope to the passions
and prejudices of those by whom they are surrounded. Soon
after the note on this subject was presented to me by Monsieur Del Campo an application was received from the
Comte d'Artois praying His Majesty's assistance to transport
himself into Brittany, and to maintain himself there. The
answer . . . was favourable, tho' not conclusive. We expressing an inclination on His Majesty's part to comply with
the request, but stating the necessity of previous explanation . . . . . You will communicate these particulars to the
Court of Madrid as forming the answer to the proposal made
by that Government on the subject of Monsieur, and as
manifesting the King's disposition to concur with His Catholic Majesty by every means in His Power for the promotion
of those salutary objects which the two courts have in view."
In another letter of the same date Grenville wrote :[1]

[1] Record Office.

" In addition to what I have already written to your Excellency on the subject of Toulon I am now to mention a circumstance respecting that place which his Majesty has seen with much concern. A letter for his Majesty from the Comte de Provence was yesterday delivered to me by the duke d'Harcourt. By the copy which I enclose to your Excellency of this letter you will see that in it, the Comte de Provence announces to the King, as a resolution already taken, His design of going to Toulon, and that he takes upon himself to say that he goes there to exercise the Functions of Regent, and I am informed that he is actually set out upon this journey. If no other considerations had prevailed, the respect due to His Majesty required that no steps should be taken by Monsieur with regard to Toulon, without first submitting it to His Majesty's consideration & decision. The Question whether the Comte de Provence should go there at all, in the present moment, is one worthy of much deliberation. His going there as regent, while the place is in its present situation, is liable to still more question; but attempting to take these steps without the King's previous consent while the Port and Town of Toulon are held by His Majesty and occupied by His Forces, cannot in any manner be permitted. It is proper that I should not conceal from Y. Exy. the suspicion entertained here that this step has been secretly suggested or at least encouraged by the Court of Spain, as one, the success of which would tend to increase their influence in Toulon. The Possibility of this only increases the necessity of your holding a firm and decided language both as to the absolute command to be exercised at Toulon by Governor O'Hara, as also to this particular Point of Monsieur's admission there. Information having been, some time since, received which seemed to make it not improbable that Monsieur would take the step, which he has now announced, provisional orders were put to his Majesty's Officers at Toulon directing them not to admit of Monsieur's coming there, without His Majesty's previous consent being signified to them, and measures were taken to prevent the eclat which a public demand and refusal on this subject might produce, by previously apprising Monsieur of the embarrassment to which such an event would expose him. I have now taken further steps for this purpose, but as they may fail in their effect I have received the King's orders expressly to instruct Y. Exy. to represent, in the strongest terms, to the Spanish government the disrespectful conduct of Monsieur toward His Majesty on this occasion, and to announce to them the orders which His Majesty has thought proper in consequence of it, to send to Gov. O'Hara positively prohibiting him from suffering Monsieur to enter Toulon. In your communication on this subject you will not appear to believe that the Spanish government could be in any way a party to this inconsiderate and improper step on the part of Monsieur. But you will remark that this instance of disrespect towards the King obliges him to suspend the discussions which he had been willing to open with Monsieur, respecting the recognition of His claim to the Regency of France, according to the desire which had been expressed by the Court of Madrid. You may however add that His Majesty on being informed that Monsieur has abandoned his present Project and is sensible of the impropriety of his conduct towards His Majesty, will be ready to resume the consideration of that Point on the grounds which I have stated to you at large in my other letter of this day."

Before this time the agents of the Princes were active in Toulon also, and apparantly in understanding with the Spaniards. On Nov. 23 the Comité de Surveillance and the Sections of Toulon announced to Elliot their desire for the restoration of the ancient form of government, for the acknowledgment of Monsieur as Regent, and for the immediate exercise of his authority in Toulon. I shall give here the original reports relating to this question. The first is a letter from Elliot to Henry Dundas; [1] dated Toulon Nov. 24.—"I

---

[1] Record Office.

have received the enclosed paper from the Comité de Surveillance and the sections of Toulon, by which you will see how decided the public mind is at Toulon for the restoration of their ancient government. The warmth with which they desire the acknowledgment of the Regent and the immediate exercise of his authority here, without touching at all on the constitution of 1789, confirmes extremely the Idea I had formed of their dispositions. It is worthy of remark that the sections are the most popular assemblies that can be conceived, being composed without distinction of all inhabitants who think proper to attend them.—I confess that every view I have on the subject inclines me strongly to think that the acknowledgment of the Regent by all the combined Powers is a measure highly desirable. The interests of the monarchy which (though His Majesty is not ultimately pledged to that principle) we have in the meanwhile avowedly espoused, and the restoration of which, is infinitely the most important object of the war, would surely be much promoted by the advantage of an ostensible and legitimate representation of the royal authority. I am persuaded it would detach from us no support on which we can depend, and it would add a greater accession of numbers and zeal to the service. It is a measure so likely to work on the imagination of Frenchmen that one can not help considering it as at least possible, that a general and sudden turn might be given to the affairs of France by this single change in our system. I am aware that other objects may justly, and perhaps must in point of policy, as well as of fidelity to our allies, be taken into the consideration of this subject and that on these accounts, this resolution can not be adopted otherwise than in consequence of a previous discusion with the Princes, and by a general concert with the combined Powers. I am therefore glad to hear that the first steps seem to have been taken, and considering that one of our allies, the court of Spain, has already declared its sentiments, I flatter myself with the hope of the negotiation being brought to an early and favorable conclusion—the more I learn of the true nature of the counter-revolutionary spirit in France, the more I am inclined to the opinion, I have taken the liberty of delivering, and the more essential I think it to our success that the measure should be adopted. With regard to the application made to me by the sections of Toulon on this subject, I shall be able to prevent their carrying any measure into execution until I have the honor of receiving His Majesty's commands. I can not say that I see any local inconvenience in the admission of the Regent into Toulon, and the establishment of his authority here, and it might possibly produce a good effect in the adjacent country, and even in the besieging Army, at the same time it must be observed that by such a condescension His Majesty would perform his engagements for the redelivery of Toulon earlier than can be claimed by the terms of the convention : and possibly some advantage might be lost in treating for the terms of peace. But if anything were gained by it, towards accelerating the settlement of France, I confess, I should think all disadvantages on other points sufficiently compensated. There is too much reason to fear that Austria is more indifferent to the main object of the war, and more attached to points of her own, than she professes to be. Prussia we know is not to be depended on, and if Great Britain does not throw her whole weight into the scale of a more enlarged and sounder policy, there is great reason to fear for the issue of this contest."

Elliot enclosed the following: Answer of the Commissioners at Toulon to the comité de surveillance respecting the Regent.[1] 27th of Nov. " Nous avons reçu avec beaucoup d'interet la communication qui nous a été faite de vos deliberations et de celles des sections de Toulon, relativement à la Regence. Nous y reconnaissons avec le plus grand plaisir des sentiments dignes à la fois du patriotisme et de la sagesse de cette ville respectable. Nous partageons

---

[1] Record Office.

avec elle non seulement le désir de voir renaître l'ordre sous
un gouvernment fondé sur des bons principes, non seulement les sentiments de loyauté et d'attachment pour votre
jeune et infortuné monarche, mais aussi ceux du respect et
de la vénération, pour la famille de vos rois, et surtout pour
l'auguste personnage qui est l' object de vos veux. Nous
nous trouvons néanmoins dans l'impossibilité de concourir
immédiatement à l'accomplissement de vous souhaits et
nous désirons vous faire part des obstacles qui s'y opposent.
La Regence de la France interesse l'Europe entière et surtout les Puissances coalisées, puisque dans le circonstances
actuelles l'autorité du Regent comme celle du trône même
ne peut être réalisée que par leur sécours et par des efforts
immense de leur part. Cet object donc doit de toute néces-
sité, comme par toutes les obligations tante de la saine poli-
tique que des sentiments honnêtes (les seuls qui puissent
animer ces Princes illustres) être traité directement avec les
cours qui combattent les ennemis de votre Roy. Une affaire
aussi importante et qui embrasse des rélations politiques
aussi étendues et aussi combinées ne peut être terminée
avec effet ni peutêtre meme tentée avec avantage par une
seule ville respectable à la verite à toutes sortes de titres,
mais pour le moment non seulement isolée du reste de la
France, mais ayant contracté pour l' interet du royaume,
comme pour son propre salut, des rélations récentes et
sacrées avec une autre puissance. Il est evident dans tous
les cas que les ministres de sa Majesté Britannique doivent
être absolument incompetens à décider sur ces objets sans
avoir specialement consulté leur cour et obtenu des pouvoirs
directs. Tout ce qu' ils pourront faire pour seconder le zéle
louable des habitans de Toulon, est de soumettre sans delai
cette matière interessante à la sagesse et aux lumières de
Sa Majesté et d'attendre ses ordres. Jusqu'alors ne nous
trouvant point autorisés à compromettre sa Majesté sur la
question de la Regence, nous pouvons encore moins con-
sentir à la proposition qui a été faite d'appeller Monsieur le

Comte de Provence à Toulon, pour y exercer les fonctions
de Regent parce que ce serait destituer Sa Majesté Britannique avant l'epoque stipulé de l' autorité qui lui a été
dernièrement confiée à Toulon. Ces raisons ne nous obligent
cependant point de nous opposer au desir que pourraient
avoir les habitans de cette ville de parter leurs hommages
aux pieds de ce Prince et de lui exprimer tous les voeux
que doivent inspirer ses vertus personelles ou que peuvent
réclamer les droits de sa naissance.

À Toulon ce 27 de Novembre 1793. Signé; Hood, Elliot,
O'Hara.

Elliot commented on this answer in another letter to Henry
Dundas, on the same day: "We have endeavoured to con-
form ourselves to the spirit of His Majesty's commands as
conveyed in your despatch of the 22 of October. . . .
But although we have been careful not to commit His
Majesty on the question and have positively refused to admit the Princes into Toulon, without His Majesty's orders
we did not think it necessary to prevent the inhabitants
from paying to him any compliment they thought fit, or
acknowledging in their own name his right to the Regency.
We thought it might even be advantageous that they should
execute that part of their intentions because in the first
place it will unite great numbers of them in a measure in
which the constitution of 1789 is not mentioned, and in
the next place, will afford security for their steadiness, as it
renders their case more desperate with the convention." [1]

The retreat of the Allies from Toulon brought this question to an end. The English whose main object in the war
was the "indemnification" regarded a stable form of government as the necessary condition for the obtaining, as
well as for the peaceful enjoyment of, this indemnification.
Toulon they intended to hold as security for it. The interests of the French monarchy for which England had
declared principally out of consideration for Austria, and

---

[1] These three communications just given are all from the Record Office.

perhaps for her other Allies, were not thought of as sufficiently important to justify her sacrificing her authority at Toulon by the admission of Monsieur. Again, the French fleet was to be considered. Although nowhere mentioned, it is certain that the English were conscious of the fact that by the admission of Monsieur, the ships also would be under his command and consequently neither come into English hands nor even be destroyed. The removal of the fleet formed part of England's plan for supremacy in the Mediterranean. Spain, however, beside her natural inclination to aid the French princes from dynastic interests, was not at all adverse to the idea of the English authority at Toulon being superceded, more especially as her own influence would be far greater with the Regent than with the English. The Sardinian Court to which the Princes had also applied, was at this time quite subject to the interests of England. Neither from Hood's declaration which recognized the constitution of 89, nor from the King's declaration which declared for hereditary monarchy, was England under any binding moral obligation to recognize Monsieur as Regent. As a political move it is hard to say what would have been the result. In all probability Monsieur would have arrived too late to have had any material influence upon the affairs of Toulon.

The dispute as to the division of authority always remained an unsettled one. In the beginning of November St. Helens advised Alcudia to wait until he (St. Helens) received news from England and meanwhile that both Generals should command. On November 8 St. Helens wrote to Grenville: [1] "The Duke de la Alcudia has nominated M. Ocarez (who was chargé d'affaires in France, at the time of the death of the late King) to reside at Toulon as Plenipotentiary from this court; an appointment which seems to have been created in imitation of that of Sir Gilbert Elliot, however I do not find that he is invested with any similar

---

[1] Record Office.

Commission, his instructions being merely to correspond
regularly with the Department of the first secretary of State."

On November 13. St. Helens wrote further: [1] that the dispute between the admirals continued, but that Hood assured
him that it would not interfere with the cause, "O'Hara and
Gravina waving entirely the Question relative to the chief
Command:"—on November 27, that the differences were
arranged and that O'Hara was to have the chief command
of the combined forces on shore and Gravina the government of the city. Hood however was not in a very conciliatory mood especially as he had a very low opinion of the
Spanish. As early as October 11 he wrote to Trevor [2] " I
must mention to you in confidence that no dependence can
be placed in the Spanish or Neopolitians, they cannot be left
anywhere to themselves." On November 20 Elliot wrote to
St. Helens, complaining of the quality of the Spanish soldiers; [3] " It is his (O'Hara's) opinion, and I believe Lord
Hood's, that if you can by any means obtain better troops,
or if not, if you can even withdraw those that are here you
will render a service to the Garrison. . . . . . If any dis-
aster should take place here it will become a very serious
question, in what manner the French ships should be disposed of. In that event if Spain in persuance of their present
notions of *equality* should set up any claim of participation
in the possession of those ships our measures will be exposed to great Embarrassement. I need say no more to satisfy
your Lordship of the Importance of this matter and we leave
it with great confidence in your hands". This shows conclusively that even Elliot, who falsely regarded the restoration of monarchy as the principal object of the war, and who
was in favor of recognizing Monsieur as Regent, had no intention of admiting any " equality ", in fact any share, in
the distribution of the French ships. In such a state of affairs a more serious turn in the old dispute seemed inevita-

---

1 Record Office.
2 Foreign Office. Sardinia 1793. R. O.
3 Commissioners to Toulon 1793. R. O.

ble; but the position of the Allies having become gradually
quite precarious, the political questions fell into the background. Even before November 30, the English more than
doubted the strength of their hold on the town. On Nov.
23 Elliot wrote to Dundas [1] " It seems to me that the possession of this place is precarious, and that every day is critical ": the next day to Lady Elliot, "O.Hara thinks as ill as
possible of this business as it now stands; but reinforcements may be expected before the worst may happen. Lord
Hood is over confident and will never admit the slighest
doubt of our keeping the place." [2]

The English had changed their opinion on another question also. On Oct 19. Mulgrave wrote to Trevor [3] "You
must not send us one emigré of any sort; they would be a
nuisance, they are all so various and so violent in their
principles of gouvernment whether for despotism, Constitution or Republic, that we should be distracted with their
quarrels and they are so assuming, forward, dictatorial and
full of complaints, that no business could go on with them.
Lord Hood is adverse to receiving any of them. You must
therefore put them off as civilly as you can." A little more
than a month later Elliot informed Dundas [4] that they had
sent to Italy for twenty to eighty emigrant officers, and on
December 8,[5] Hood, Elliot and Dundas informed the emigrants that they might serve under their own officers, but
subject to the Government of Toulon. Not many were to
serve as officers, but principally as private soldiers which
"l' amour de la Patrie sçait concilier avec l'honneur de la
noblesse Française". They were also directed to ask the approbation of the Princes as that would help the cause. On
Dec. 18. Trevor wrote to Grenville,[6] "The emigrants wait

---

[1] Commissioners to Toulon. R. O.

[2] Life of Elliot, Minto.

[3] Sardinia, Foreign Office. R. O.

[4] Letter Nov. 27th. Commissioners to Toulon.

[5] Elliot to Trevor. Dec. 8. Foreign Office. Sardinia. R. O.

[6] Foreign Office. Sardinia. R. O.

for His Royal Highness orders before they determine upon
accepting our offers of receiving them at Toulon. I cannot
doubt but that he will tell them to go." The emigrants were
still negotiating in Switzerland when Bonaparte's batteries
had driven the Allies from Toulon. On Dec. 1. Elliot wrote
to Dundas:[1] "Nothing very important has occured in the
political affairs of this place and indeed that department is
naturally rather in the background, while our situation is so
critical". This marks the end of the dispute between the two
nations in the city itself. Other thoughts occupy their attention. Elliot wrote Dec. 9.[2] "I consider our possession of this
place very precarious, which is not surprising, considering
that I have heard that opinion from every military man of
rank since I came here": On Dec. 12. . . . . "General Dundas is in very low spirits and seems to dispond more than
ever". The tone of the two courts, especially of the Spanish,
was far from being conciliatory. The two following cum-
munications show that the disputed question bade fair to
become insoluble. The fall of Toulon rendered a solution
unnecessary.

Grenville to St. Helens. Whitehall. Dec. 1. "The original
tenor as well as the particular expressions of Monsieur Del
Campo's late notes, are so entirely inconsistent with the relations in which the two courts have been placed with respect
to each other by the late negotiations and by the circumstances which still exist that it is thought absolutely necessary that Your Excellency should ascertain whether the form
and language of those notes were prescribed to him by his
court, or whether they arise solely from ill disposition towards this country of which he has given such repeated
proofs. And if the latter should be found to be the case Your
Excellency will no doubt judge it absolutely necessary to
adopt some proper expedient by which the Duke of Alcudia
may be apprised how little Monsieur Del Campo's conduct

---

[1] Commissioners to Toulon. R. O.
[2] To Lady Elliot. Life of Elliot. Minto.

appears calculated to promote union and good understanding between the two countries."

St. Helens wrote to Grenville on Dec. 25. " But at any rate I think it my duty to acquaint your Lordship without Loss of time, that this court does not hitherto appear to be disposed to relinquish voluntarily their pretended Right to the perpetual nomination of the Commander in Chief of the combined Forces in Toulon unless it be on the evidently inadmissable condition, of their being allowed to remove from that Port and to retain under their sole Custody, the greater part, if not the whole, of the French fleet now lying there : . . . . and that they have also rendered the arrangement of this disputed point still more difficult than before by nominating to the command of the Spanish Troops at Toulon the celebrated Count O'Reilly who (not to mention the objections that might be stated against his personal character and dispositions) is a Lieutenant General of near 30 years standing and consequently superior in Point of seniority to any officer of that Rank in the British Army ".

One other question which preoccupied the British cabinet during the entire siege was that of the Austrian reinforcements. In the *rapprochement* between London and Vienna which came about in the War of the First Coalition, and which had by the publication of the King's Declaration taken the form of an explicit policy of " indemnification ", the English court had expected the assistance of from 12 to 15,000 Austrian troops for any offensive operations which might take place from the Mediterranean. On hearing of the surrender of Toulon, Pitt wrote to Grenville telling him to press the Emperor to send troops, and on Sep. 14 such instructions were sent to Eden. As early as Sep. 11 Eden informed Grenville[1] that he had demanded troops from Thugut, who made excuses saying that they were needed on the Rhine, and complaining of the backwardness of Prussia. On Sept. 25 Eden wrote that he urged that a force should be sent to Toulon and Thugut replied that he would recom-

[1] Austria. Sir Morton Eden. Record Office.

mend it to His Majesty. But at the same time Eden wrote
to Trevor telling him that the troops were coming; as if it
had been already settled. Austria did promise the troops
however, but under conditions. Eden wrote to Auckland[1]
"This country gives *us* 5000 men . . . but will not allow
them to be employed offensively to make conquests for the
King of Sardinia unless that Sovereign will (if any are made)
yield them, though in a very inferior proportion something
in return for the share of this court in the Novarese".
Thaon de Revel says in his Memoirs; "Les troupes autrich-
iennes qui étaient dans les garnisons de l'état de Milan y
étaient restées paisiblement au lieu de marcher sur Lyon, ce
qui en eut empêché la chute et porté un coup mortel à la
revolution. L'Angleterre demandait que les Autrichiens
reunis aux Piedmontais chassassent les Français du comté
de Nice d'une partie de la Provence et que l'on entr'ouvrît
une communication directe et sure avec Toulon. L'appre-
hension de la Cour de Vienne que le Roi de Sardaigne n'eut
des succès, s'opposa dans cette occasion comme dans toutes
les autres à tout ce que le lien commun de la coalition con-
seillait si fortement. Elle espérait que si le Roi de Sardaigne
se trouvait dans l'embarras il consentirait à lui ceder une
partie des acquisitions faites anciennement sur l'état de
Milan."

This jealousy of Sardinia, a distrust of England and a
failing to see any tangible and immediate gain were the
real reasons why Austria did not send the troops. The
reasons she put forward were others.[2] On Oct. 30 Eden
wrote: [3] " In a conversation with the Austrian minister he
repeated with some appearance of alarm the danger of their
present situation unsupported by Prussia and the Dutch and
their numbers reduced by repeated losses, particularly in
the affair before Maubeuge, and asked me if in the case

---

1 Correspondence of Auckland.

2 On Nov. 4. Thugut received information from London "assez propre
à calmer nos inquiétudes sur les intentions des Anglais relativement à
Dunkerque." Vertrauliche Briefe von Thugut. von Vivenot.

3 Eden to Grenville R. O.

Toulon should be found from the reinforcements already arrived there not to stand in need of the troops promised from
hence."

The troops were looked for at Toulon and Hood dis-
patched Admiral Goodal to Genoa to bring them but the
ships returned as empty as the departed. Finally however
the English Cabinet, impatient at this delay, assumed more
and more express terms in demanding the troops, as the following instructions to Eden will show. They are dated
Nov. 11. [1] " You will remonstrate in the strongest terms
against this delay as a positive breach of faith and as likely
to be in its consequences highly injurious to the common interests." . . . Nov. 24.[1] " You will therefore now admit
of no further excuse but formally claim the immediate
execution of the engagement and lose no time in apprizing
me of the result." On Dec. 8 Eden replied [1] " I called
on Thugut . . . . and in obedience to your Lordship's express directions demanded, in His Majesty's
name, an order for the immediate march of the reinforcements promised to His Majesty for the support of Toulon."
It was not until Dec. 16. that Eden was finally able to
assure John Trevor that [2] "every Difficulty is removed " and
" that His Imperial Majesty has issued his orders for the
immediate march of the troops for Toulon." This time the
Austrians were undoubtedly sincere but as is seen, it was
too late. Before this note could reach Trevor, Toulon was
lost. The English had been over-confident at Toulon. Although Dundas, the secretary of war, had been repeatedly
warned, he could not realize that it was possible to lose the
place. He counted too much on the bad quality of the Republicans. As late as Dec. 27. troops were being em-
barked at Cork for Toulon, [3] and but a few days before Pay-
master General Lennox was sent from London.[4]

<hr>

[1] Record Office.
[2] Letters from Dundas. British Museum. Mss. Additional 27, 594.
[3] War Office Letter Books. Commander-in-chief. (1792–94) R. O.
[4] Admiralty Records, War Office. (1782–1794). Dec. 20. R. O.

CHAPTER III.

NEWS OF THE FALL OF TOULON IN SPAIN, FRANCE AND ENG-
LAND—RESULTS OF THE FALL OF TOULON—FATE OF
SHIPS AT TOULON—ROLE OF BONAPARTE—MEMOIRES
OF BARRAS—INFLUENCE OF THE SIEGE ON BONAPARTE.

The news of the fall of Toulon caused in republican
France and especially in Paris, the wildest joy. On Dec. 24.
it was announced by Barrère in the Convention. At the same
time he made a motion that " L'armée dirigée contre Toulon
a bien mérité de la Patrie." The entire assembly arose with
loud shouts of approbation. A few days later Robespierre
began one of his long speeches with, " laissons l'Europe et
l'histoire vanter les miracles de Toulon et préparons de nou-
veaux triomphes à la liberté ". The Convention decided to
declare a general holiday and on Dec. 30. the great " fête de
rejouissance " took place. David was ordered to prepare it.
The entire Convention took part in the tremendous proces-
sion. For weeks the Theaters gave popular performances
" en rejouissence de la reprise de Toulon," and " La prise de
Toulon " was often read in the papers of that time as the
title to a play which was supposed to win popular favor.
Not only in Paris and in France, but even in America and
in Constantinople one celebrated the fall of Toulon. As to
the reception of the news in Spain, St. Helens wrote on January 8.[1] " With regard to the sensations produced here by
the late abandonment of Toulon it seems to me that if this
court feel any concern on that account it arises rather from
certain collateral considerations than from their conceiving
that event to be in itself prejudicial to the common interests . . . . . they are of the opinion that by the destruction of the arsenal and shipping of Toulon we have secured
all the essential advantages which the surrender of that place
was ever likely to have afforded without the Burthen and

---

[1] Record Office.
2192—7

Risk of maintaining possession of it, this seems to be likewise the opinion of the public at large ". Lord St. Helen's
opinion was corroborated by the Gazetta de Madrid which
gave the accounts of the evacuation. But from now on, an
enmity gradually developed between England and Spain,
and in the Declaration of War by Spain in 1796 is found
the following passage " This ill faith became manifest in
the most critical moment of the 1st. campagne from the
manner in which Lord Hood treated my fleet at Toulon
where he attended to nothing but the destruction of what he
could not carry away with him." As the Spaniards were by
no means an inactive party to the destruction referred to,
this passage is open to some criticism; but it shows none
the less that the differences between the English and Spanish left some impression. Later on it was even stated openly
in London that the Spanish blew up the ships in the harbor
of Toulon purposely to destroy the English boats. This statement is no doubt false, but it shows to what extent the ill
feeling between the two countries went.

In England the news was received with surprise but with
no great amount of disappointment. The Opposition welcomed it however as they hoped to use it against the government. Nelson's opinion was in general the most prevalent one.[1] " For England the getting rid of such a place is
a most happy event. Our money would have gone very fast.
The quitting of Toulon by us I am satisfied is a national
benefit ". The Earl of Elgin wrote to Grenville on the[2] " un-
fortunate news " but added " the destroying the fleet and
arsenal and saving the garrison are great palliatives ". At
the opening of Parliament on Jan. 21, 1794. the following
reference is made to Toulon, in the King's speech: " the
temporary possession of the town and post of Toulon has
greatly distressed the operations of my enemies; and in the
circumstances attending the evacuation of that place an im-

---

1 Nelson's Dispatches.

2 Elgin to Grenville. Dec. 29. Fortesque Mss.

portant and decisive blow has been given to their naval
power, by the distinguished conduct, abilities and spirit of my
commanders, officers and forces both by sea and by land ".
This was to a great extent the opinion in official circles.
Lord Star in the address of thanks replied "Since the mem-
orable battle of La Hogue a more brilliant enterprise had
not been achieved than that at Toulon by Lord Hood. The
destruction of the Arsenal and naval stores of the second sea-
port of France was a circumstance that she could not repair
for years. It must necessarily cripple her navy for the present and for years to come and prove the most fatal blow
that was struck at the French marine". The Opposition in
Parliament however used the affair at Toulon as an opportunity of condemning the conduct as well as the object of
the war. Fox was especially bitter in his criticism, while
Pitt defended the government. On the opening of the session
in Jan. 94. in his attack upon the government Fox referred
frequently to Toulon. " When we have been driven from
Toulon in a manner so afflicting if not disgraceful " . . . .
He then pointed out the difference between the object of
gaining "some solid advantage for ourselves, as an indemnification for the expenses of the war and that of giving
such a government to France as ministers might think it
safe to treat with" . . . . "Toulon was taken by the
British in consequence of certain conditions stipulated by
the inhabitants. And yet even with the certainty of the
guillotine before them these inhabitants were so unwilling
to assist the British, that no other than an ignominious evacuation could be effected. If it was right so to take it, it became a matter of indespensible duty to defend it. Toulon,
purchased by compromise you have lost with disgrace; you
have placed yourselves in a point of view entirely new to
British character, you have proved yourselves neither useful as friends, nor respectable as enemies ". On May. 30. in
speaking of the King's declaration he said; "A declaration
in the name of his majesty afterwards came out different

indeed from this: verbose, obscure and equivocal like the production of men who are afraid of saying anything distinctly, who wish not their meaning to be clearly understood: that stript of all the elegant rubbish with which it was loaded declared only this, that the restoration of monarchy without specifying what kind, was the only condition upon which we could treat with France". Pitt replied; "the right honorable gentleman proceeded to bring forward a charge of inconsistency from the declaration of Lord Hood at Toulon and that afterwards published by His Majesty, addressed to the people of France. These declarations, I affirm, are perfectly consistent. That of Lord Hood only promises protection to the people of Toulon, as far as he could grant it without specifying any particular form of government they chose to pledge themselves to the Constitution of 1789. The declaration of His Majesty offers protection to all the people of France, who shall approve of an hereditary monarchy". Pitt was not quite honest here as he gave rather how he wished Hood's declaration should be interpreted, than how it was in reality. It will be remembered that the English government was not satisfied with it. The affair of Toulon remained however a favourite point of attack for Fox, and as late as March. 95 he made allusion to it.

From a military stand-point the results of the fall of Toulon were the following. First. The moral effect of the expulsion of the combined forces of four nations from the soil of France was great. Second. The large army employed at Toulon was now free to swell the ranks of the armies of Alpes and of the Pyrenees; the friends of royalty in the south of France had no longer a "*point d'appui*" in Toulon, and the barbarous punishment of the rebellious city could not but have its effect upon other cities with similar intentions. Third. The occupation of Toulon by the Allies had struck a severe blow at the French navy, a very large part of which was stationed here. It was of this fact that the

English most boasted and with which they consoled themselves for the forced evacuation. Of the 31 ships of line in the harbor, 11 were burnt, 4 sent away with the French seamen at the begining of the siege (this caused a good deal of criticism in England), 3 were carried off by the English and the rest saved, thanks to the rapid advance of the Republicans on the last two days of the siege. Of the 12 frigates, 5 entered the service of the English, 1 was given to Sardinia, 3 burnt and the rest saved by the Republicans. There were 13 corvettes of which 7 went to England, 1 to Spain, 1 to Naples, 2 burnt and the rest saved by the Republicans. As is seen, the English received about all the ships. They were taken to be guarded for the King of France: which meant that the English had the use of them until the Restoration, 20 years afterwards. She then made excuses for keeping those of them which were left at that time. Besides the ships, the yards and naval stores of all kinds were destroyed at Toulon; but the large guns, as well as the fortifications erected by the Allies themselves, could not be destroyed for want of time. Bonaparte rejoicing over this fact wrote on Dec. 24. "Toulon est plus dans le cas de se défendre aujourd'hui que jamais."

As to the historical significance of the affair of Toulon, its fall was one of the most important successes of the Republicans which rendered the peace of Campo Formio possible; its occupation by the Allies was the occasion of England's forming a brilliant scheme of indemnification, which expressed her intentions during the War of the First Coalition. But the siege of Toulon will be known principally as the action in which Napoleon first distinguished himself. The exact part which he played in this important event has become a question of dispute, giving rise to various opinions. After studying the question I have become convinced and hope to be able to prove that those who attribute to Napoleon a great part in the success of the Republican Army are quite right. The grounds upon which they base their opinion may often be false however. It has frequently been said that Napoleon alone, with the eye of a genius, discovered the one vulnerable point in the outskirts of Toulon, namely the Eguillette, and by this one act decided the fate of the city. This is false. He choose, as any other well schooled officer would have done, the Eguillette as a point of attack, but he is entitled to no great credit for having done so. Again according to his own statement and to that of the Representatives, this plan corresponded practically with that sent on from Paris; and again, the Allies themselves recognized the importance of this point, and seized and fortified it before the Republicans could take advantage of it. This was due to the slowness of Carteaux. The great merit of Bonaparte lay in the fact that he alone organized and commanded the artillery, which at all sieges and most especially at Toulon, played the important part. Bonaparte showed the greatest activity in the equiping as well as in the direction of this arm. Even many of the officers were called to Toulon by him personally. He showed excellent judgement in placing his batteries; so much so that, as has been seen, the shots from the first one erected, after Bonaparte had been but a few days at Toulon, announced to the Allies the possibility of their being forced to evacuate the place. The notes of the Spanish Minster, of the English ambassador at Madrid, and of Hood are eloquent proofs of this. Almost up to the end the Republican Army was in a most deplorable state. The Artillery was the one redeeming feature, the one arm which gave the Allies any concern. All their sallies were made in order to destroy the steadily approaching batteries. The daring and disasterous sortie in which O'Hara was captured, was rendered necessary by the opening of the fire of the *Convention*. The great part which the artillery played in the final attack on Eguillette has been seen. The shots from the newly erected batteries were what forced the Allies to hasten their retreat on the last day, and consequently made it impossible for them to complete their work

of burning the ships and yards. In fact the proofs of the
great activity of the artillery stand out in vivid contrast to
the inefficiency of the other branches of the army. The artillery was entirely the work of Bonaparte; he had the sole
command until the arrival of Du Thiel, and the real command even then, for Du Theil was old, ailing and could
not take any active part. The council of war had approved
all the batteries erected by Bonaparte, and the positions of
all those erected after Du Theil's arrival had been chosen
by Napoleon; and most of them already commenced. Du
Theil was brave, well instructed and made a good impression
on Dugommier. He recognised immediately the talent of
Bonaparte as is shown by the following lines written to the
Minister of war on the day of the entrance of the Republicans in Toulon.[1] "Je manque d'expression pour te peindre le
mérite de Bonaparte; beaucoup de science, autant d'intelligence, et trop de bravour, voilà une faible esquisse des vertus
de ce rare officier. C'est à toi citoyen ministre de les con-
sacrer à la Gloire de la République." Victor wrote in his
Memoirs; "Or ces puissantes moyens (the artillery) étaient
dirigés par Bonaparte; car le general Dutheil émerveillé de
la justesse et de la superiorité de ses vues s'était complète-
ment effacé devant lui; noble et rare abnégation! hommage
magnifique qui honore à la fois celui qui le rendait et celui
qui en fut l'objet". The Duc de Raguse wrote in his Memoirs; "Duthiel fut venu pour prendre le commandement
en chef de l'Artillerie. Celui-ci vit le pouvoir en si bonnes
mains et si bien exercé et les commandements avaient sou-
vent alors des conséquences si graves qu'il laissa faire le
jeune officier et ne prit aucune part à la direction du siège."
He made the same statement as Victor, but attributed Du
Thiel's action to different motives. His implying that Du
Thiel feared the responsibility of the command is no doubt
unjust. General Doppet said in his Memoirs, written in
1797; "Duthiel fit avec moi la visite des batteries établies

---

[1] War Archives. These lines have been frequently published.

avant mon arrivé et je vis avec autant d'étonnement et de satisfaction que cet ancien Artilleur applaudit à toutes les mesures qu'avait prit le jeune Bonaparte." Many other less important proofs are found in the writings of those who took part in the siege. Carteaux's final praise of the Artillery and Dugommier's and Salicetti's special mention of Bonaparte during the siege have already been spoken of.

Barras also wrote in his Memoirs on the siege of Toulon, and it is principally upon his writings that those who deny the importance of Bonaparte's role, base their opinion. That Barras' Memoires are hostile to Napoleon is admitted by all who know them. That Barras' account of the siege of Toulon is full of mistakes and consequently almost worthless as a source, will be seen by everybody who compares it with any trustworthy acount of the siege. And yet he tried to demonstrate that Bonaparte's role at Toulon was only secondary. It seems to me that he has really proved the contrary. Here are a few of his sentences. " Des sa première recontre avec moi je fut frappé de son activité". . . . "je lui donnai devant tout le monde des preuves de ma ·bienviellance". . . . " Bientot admis à ma table il fut toujours placé à coté de moi ". . . . " Dugommier accorda *de suite* la plus grande confiance à celui qu'il appelait " mon petit protègé ". Bonaparte ne tarda pas à en abuser; il prit bientot un ton absolute et décisif qui déplut au general en chef ". . . . " Bonaparte commandait l'artillerie provisoirement. Ce n'etait pas assez pour lui de ce commandement important, il fallait qu'il se mélâ de tout et de tout le monde ". These lines show that Napoloen made himself everywhere conspicuous. The hostile tone of the same may easily be attributed to Barras' prejudice, Further he continued. " Bonaparte donna quelques prouves de son talent militaire qui commençait à se developper; mais il n'agit que secondairement dans cette circonstance : je le répète le veritable " preneur" de Toulon, c'est Dugommier." When one recalls the fact that on the 13th. Vendémiaire Barras placed his entire fortune in the hands of Bonaparte, and a few days later said to the Convention, "J'attirai l'attention de la Convention nationale sur le général Buona Parte, c'est lui, c'est à ses dispositions savantes et promptes qu'on doit la defense de cette enciente autour de laquelle il avait distribué des postes avec beaucoup d'habilite ", (he then proposed him for "général en second de l'armée de l'interieur ") and when one remembers that Barras was largely instrumental in procuring for Bonaparte the command of the army of Italy, one is justified in believing that his opinion of Bonaparte at this time was somewhat different from that at the time he wrote his Memoires. Barras' contempory opinion of Dugommier has been preserved and differs much from that which he gave in his Memoires. On Nov. 29. he wrote to the Comité du Salut Public "La situation de l'armée n'est pas satisfaisante. Je suis loin d'inculper le général Dugommier. Cependent ce général questionné par moi n'a pu me dire le nombre de troupes qu'il commande; il ignore le nom des bataillons arrivées, le nom et le nombre de ceux qu'il attend ; il n'avait encore fait ni fait faire aucune revue, il ne connaissait pas la situation de ses principales batteries ; je l'ai exhorté à s'occuper plus serieusement de la grande affaire dont vous l'avez chargé et de surveiller toutes les parties de l'administration qui m'ont paru très negligées; il m'a tout promis ; il m'a paru très bien intentioné, puisse-t-il tenir parole ". Barras' opinion of Dugommier may be of no great value but it seems strange to see him write in this tone of him whom he afterwards termed the "veritable preneur de Toulon." Further he wrote. "La prise du général O'Hara attribué à Bonaparte, le vaiseau qu'il aurait coulé bas, le plan de campagne auquel il aurait participé sont autont d'assertions fausses, imaginées par celui qui en a imaginé bien d'autres, répétées par ses flatteurs le jour où il a eu l'argent pour les payer." These lines show the style and spirit in which Barras wrote of Napoleon. The statements are quite false. It is true that Bonaparte did not personally take O'Hara prisoner, and he nowhere said that he did. It is however practically certain that he commanded the body of troops who found the wounded English General. As for the "vaisseau anglais," he sank several shortly after his arrival at Toulon, as has been seen. As for the plan of attack, it has been shown how he selected it as the proper one from the very first and followed it up to the end. Barras' ideas on the proper manner of attacking Toulon I have found in a letter written by him at that time, and as it is unpublished I have given it in full. (see Appendix II) Reading it one cannot but admit that it is merely a mass of phrases put together by one who feels he is bound to say something on a subject of which he knows little. It shows that Barras is not a military man : consequently his opinion of Bonaparte's participation in a plan which he himself did not appreciate, is worthless. On Nov. 29. he wrote of the plan decided upon by the council of war. . . . . "Je l'ai trouvé très bien écrit, fort bien rédigé, même assez bien concu." Again nothing but phrases, where Barras' criticises the handwriting and literary merit of a military plan. It must surely be admitted that to judge of Napoleon's role at the siege of Toulon from Barras' memoires is quite untrustworthy, in fact worse, as they are incorrect and biased. Others[1] who have written on this event, say that nothing in the official records shows the great role played by Bonaparte. It is true that in the War Archives in Paris there is no exact statement, nor is it mathematically demonstrated that Bonaparte played the principal part in the siege of Toulon : but indirect proofs abound even here and are also to be found in the sources of the English and of the other Allies. History is not an exact science ; therefore a fact which, even through an indirect proof appeals to the reason of an unprejudiced person is taken as truth. It is quite as wrong to deny a fact which is clear, as to assert one which is false. Toulon was Bonaparte's opportunity and he took every advantage of it.

---

[1] Jung ; Krebs and Morris.

It is instructive to follow as closely as the material permits, Bonaparte's actions during these three important months: to see how during this time of jealousy, distrust and open enmity between the different officers, and between the commanding officer and Representatives, Bonaparte understood how to remain on excellent terms with them all and to continue his part of the undertaking, conscious of his aim and uninterrupted in his progress. Napoleon, spured on by his restless ambition and armed with an excellent technical instruction, needed yet something more to forward him in his wonderful career; to keep him on the proper path, and from wasting his untiring energy against impossibilities. He needed a broad knowledge of men and a clear insight into the conditions of his day. Without this he might have been a Hoche, a Kleber or a Ney, but never a Napoleon nor even a Bernadotte. His intuitive genius could not of itself have supplanted such knowledge; it made him quick in comprehending, arranging and generalizing his experience, but the experience itself was necessary. Napoleon may have needed less than others, but he needed some. Such an experience of the world of his day could not have been acquired in an artillery school in Brienne, nor in the little Island of Corsica, dealing with a unique people, nor had Bonaparte obtained it as yet in France. His *Souper de Beaucaire* shows that his views and ideas were still limited. It is first at Toulon that he acquired this broader and valuable experience. Here he took an active and important part, right in the center of an event of European importance. He was in touch with revolutionary France, with the representatives, and generals; an interested spectator of party strife and of the conflict of political and social ideas. He came into contact with the European nations, lived in an atmosphere of uncertainty, danger and intrigue. Even from a military stand-point he must have learned a great deal. Here he witnessed the combined action of the different arms, with a preponderance of his own special one. He real-

ized the importance of that department which provides for
the provisioning of the army. All this must have made a
vivid and lasting impression on the mind of Bonaparte,
then a young man, awaiting an opportunity. How well he
understood human nature is demonstrated by the tact with
which he won the confidence of all those with whom he
came in contact, the Representatives, among them Barras;
the Generals Dutheil, Doppet and Dugommier. His naming
an exposed battery in which the gunners hesitated to serve,
La batterie des Hommes-sans peur, and in this way so touching their pride that everyone strove for the honor of serving
in it, shows how well he understood his soldiers. One is re-
minded of his address to his army in Italy two years later.
Napoleon made many friends at Toulon; among them several
of his future lieutenants, Junot, Marmont, Victor and others.
His relations with the younger of the Robespierres nearly
dragged him down in their fall, and it was undoubtedly
here that arose the enmity between Napoleon and his coun-
tryman Arena who was afterwards executed for an attempt
on the life of the First Consul. But these were exceptions.
It was certainly not at Toulon that he won the hatred of
Barras; quite the contrary. Men as well as conditions he
used to his best advantage. Yet one cannot accuse him of
ingratitude. All of those who still lived when he was in
power, and the sons and grandsons of those who did not
were rewarded; many of them in his will from St. Helena.
It is a grand sight to see how the dethroned Emperor recalls and rewards those who helped him in his early career.
All this experience, good luck and self-satisfaction was no
doubt what made Napoleon feel that his history should
begin with the siege of Toulon. Yet he seemed to forget
that his thoughts, sentiments and actions before this period
were also of great interest to those who wished to study the
career of one of the world's exceptional men.

APPENDIX I.

[Record Office.]

Trevor to Grenville. TURIN Dec. 14.

—— — —— — — Monsieur is expected here the 16th
and your Lordship may depend on a faithful Execution of
the Instructions therein alluded to, the Importance of which
I see in the strongest sense and the more so because sus-
picions I have for sometime entertained are more than ever
confirmed that the Spaniards are at the bottom of a secret
intrigue of placing Monsieur at Toulon in his Character of
Regent. Your Lordship heard enough of their Behavior at
Toulon to conceive what suggestisns and what hopes their
jealousy and disappointed Pride may have given birth to.
The Princes of the blood have had some secret agents at
Toulon and I learn from thence in a private Letter of the
seventh Instant that His Majesty's commissaries knew nothing of Monsieur's Journey towards that place that the Spaniards had found means to gain a Party amongst the sections
and that a sort of wish had been expressed by them that
Monsieur should be called there as regent that this Idea
had been communicated to Sir Gilbert Elliot and that he did
not seem to consider it liable to any great inconvenience.
. . . . . If it is indeed true the dispositions at Toulon are
such, a part of our objections would be removed but there
still remains others which I shall consider as an Insult, till
I receive from your Lordship positive orders to the Contrary; and first the surreptitious manner in which it appears
to be conducted and the want of any previous application
for His Majesty's Permission which was equally necessary
from a Principle both of Policy and Respect and secondly
the weighty consideration that it is not enough that this
measure should be thought politic by the Inhabitants of
Toulon. It must also be considered so by His Majesty's
Ministers and as consistent with those Principles which
constitute the wish for the support of a vigorous government."

APPENDIX II.

[Archives Nationales.]

Paul Barras à ses collegues à Ollioules.

J'ai reflechi mes chers collegues sur le plan d'attaque proposé par le general et approuvé par vous. je crois devoir vous reiterer par ecrit et pour l'interet de la Republique une partie de mes observations. Les deux divisions de l'ouest et de l'est dirigées contre Toulon doivent attaquer dans toute leur étendu tous les postes des ennemis, parmis ces attaques il en est d'effective et de fausses. J'ose croire d'abord que les principales de ces attaques doivent être diriger contre Pharon, la chartreuse l'aiguillette ou Balaguier et Malbousquet. Deux attaques que je regarde comme decisives et devant produire subitement la prise de Toulon si elles reuississent sont celles de Pharon et de Malbosquet. Je pense donc qu'il faut surtout s'attacher plus particulairement à la pris de ses deux pósitions et que les colonnes ou les differentes corps destinés pour ces deux attaques doivent être nombreuses et bien choisis. Je pense que les aproches doivent être faites avant le jour et le lendemain d'une grande canonade qui aura démonté les canons de l'enemie et demoli ses travaux. Je pense qu'il doit être defendu de tirer un seul coup de fusil, qu'il faut joindre l'ennemi et user de l'arme blanche, qu l'impetuosité francaise rend presque toujours favorables. Je pense qu'il faut aussi prevoir tous les cas; que le resultat des attaques les mieux conbinées est quelque fois contrarié et qu'alors des pointes de ralliement doivent être convenues; des lignes ou retranchements élevés pour y recevoir les troupes repoussés ou poursuivis ainsi que des pieces de position placées dans ces retranchements. Je pense qu'il faut choisir les travailleurs et preparer en abbondance tout ce qui sera necessaire pour se loger et se retrancher aussitôt qu'on sera maitre de quelque poste ennemie. Si des postes et Pharon surtout sont pris le general doit s' attendre à de grands efforts de la parte des ennemis

pour reprendre ces positions d'ou depend leur salut; il doit
en consequence s'y fortifier sur le champ y caserner des
troupes sures et nombreuses, en longer meme sur les derri-
eres pour les appeller au besoin. Pour attaquer à la fois une
lingue aussi étendue que celle de la droite de la rade de
Toulon à sa gauche il faut de bonnes troupes. je suis d'avis
d'attaquer sans retárd mais je tiens à ce que 6000 soient sur
le champ détachés de l'armée d'Italie et envoyé sur Toulon
alors je ne considere plus le succes de l' attaque projettée
comme incertaine, alors je n'hesite plus d'assurer que les
infames brigands renferés dans Toulon n'auront autre parti
que la fuite et la mort qui les poursuivera. Quelles sont les
forces effectives de l'armée de la Republique sous les murs
de Toulon? quelest le nombre des bataillons qui les compo-
sent? je n'ai pu avoir à cet égard qu'une donnée aproxima-
tive qui la porte à 30,000 hommes et parmi laquelle on
peut compter moitie de p.requisition. Si l'ennemi a 15, 18
ou vingt mille hommes, car je n'ai encore à cet egard aucune
certitude vous hasardez peutêtre en attaquant de cette manière non seulement le sort de l'armée francaise mais celui
du midi; vous perdez au moins l'espoir d' entreprendre de
nouvelles attaques et vous êtes obligés d'attendre les forces
et l'attirail immense, mais necessaire pour faire un siège
auquel l'ennemi aura tout le temps de se preparer. observez
encore que par la distance et la nature de vos positions il
est impossible qu'elles se soutienent et se protegent mutuelle-
ment. L'armée d'Italie est fermée par les neiges, le tableau
que nous en a fait Dugomier est très rassurant. 6000
hommes de troupes experimentées et agueries en seroient
detachées pour l'attaque de Toulon. cela nous donnerait
alors une masse de force une préponderance une confiance
même à nos troupes qui nous assure du succès. Ces 6000
hommes seroient remplacés à l'armee d'Italie par des bataillons de premiere requisition, ainsi nul inconvenient d'executer de suite cete mesure. Je vous soumis de nouveau toutes
ces observations peser les dans votre sagesse communiquez

les au général, ne perdez pas de vue que la destruction de Toulon tient au salut du midi qu'il n'est aucun sacrifice aucune consideration qui doivent vous arrêter lorsque il est question de chasser l'ennemi de ce post important observez aussi qu'alors vous pourrez disposer d'une armée victorieuse et sauver la Republique en admettant tous les moyens que je vous ai demontré. Au reste il faut que Toulon soit attaqué et qu'il le soit vigoreusement si mes observations sont rejettées je me rendrai à l'armée et avec nos propres moyens nous executerons le plan proposé.

A Marseille le 8 frimaire l'an 2 de la Republique.

PAUL BARRAS.

Contents.

PART I.

Chapter I.

Chapter II.

Chapter III.

PART II.